The Profit Principle

How to turn what you know into what you do
— without spending (or borrowing) a cent!

Peter Fritz &
Jeanne-Vida Douglas

Wrightbooks

First published 2010 by Wrightbooks
an imprint of John Wiley & Sons Australia, Ltd
42 McDougall Street, Milton Qld 4064
Office also in Melbourne

Typeset in Berkeley LT 12/15.4 pt

© Peter Fritz and Jeanne-Vida Douglas 2010

The moral rights of the authors have been asserted

National Library of Australia Cataloguing-in-Publication entry:

Author:	Fritz, Peter, 1943–
Title:	The profit principle: How to turn what you know into what you do — without spending (or borrowing) a cent! / Peter Fritz and Jeanne-Vida Douglas.
ISBN:	9781742468310 (pbk.)
Notes:	Includes index.
Subjects:	Success in business—Handbooks, manuals, etc.
	Small business—Handbooks, manuals, etc.
Other Authors/ Contributors:	Douglas, Jeanne-Vida.
Dewey Number:	650.1

Cover design by Peter Reardon, Pipeline Design <www.pipelinedesign.com.au>

Printed in China by Printplus Limited

10 9 8 7 6 5 4 3 2 1

Disclaimer

The material in this publication is of the nature of general comment only, and does not represent professional advice. It is not intended to provide specific guidance for particular circumstances and it should not be relied on as the basis for any decision to take action or not take action on any matter which it covers. Readers should obtain professional advice where appropriate, before making any such decision. To the maximum extent permitted by law, the authors and publisher disclaim all responsibility and liability to any person, arising directly or indirectly from any person taking or not taking action based upon the information in this publication.

Contents

About the authors

Peter Fritz was born in 1943 in the historic city of Arad in Transylvania, during the Second World War. Following the war, his city became part of the People's Republic of Romania, and he grew up a proud and feisty pioneer. But the injustices and persecutions of the communist government weighed heavily on his family and in late 1961, after 14 years of waiting for a permit to leave the country, they made their way to Australia. Peter began working as a cleaner, studied English and later attended university part time. By the late 1960s, he found himself working in the newly emerging field of computer science.

In 1971 the company he was working for was forced to close by creditors, and, rather than lose his job, he used what he knew to launch a new company with some like-minded peers.

Forty years and a hugely successful career as an entrepreneur later, having co-founded a $1.25 billion company that employs 6000 people worldwide, he wanted to gather his experiences in business into a book so he could hand his expertise down to his children. He began to look for a writing partner, someone who also wanted to share what they knew with others, and after asking around, a friend and business associate suggested he meet Jeanne-Vida Douglas.

A multi–award winning business journalist with a decade's experience covering the information technology sector, Jeanne-Vida was looking for a way to gather together the very best stories she came across in her work into a single edition. At the time Jeanne-Vida was juggling her own small business as a freelance journalist and business writer with the demands of two small children, and was keen to encourage others to find ways to turn their skills into microenterprises.

The pair met in early 2007 at Peter's offices in Chippendale in Sydney, Jeanne-Vida bouncing her baby son on her lap, and they agreed to meet regularly for coffee to figure out how to turn these ideas and real life experiences into a book that could be shared down the generations and across the business community. Over many meetings they gathered ideas, wrote and rewrote, discussed and argued the fundamental ideas and real life examples that now fill this book.

Acknowledgements

We would like to thank Tamara Plakalo for suggesting we meet to share a common interest in business and books, Carolyn Crowther and Allison Hiew for providing us with sage advice and insightful editing, as well as Catherine Fritz-Kalish, Carla Fritz-Cordone, Sally Rose and Olga Bodrova for wading their way through early drafts, and Katherine Drew for agreeing to publish this book.

We are grateful to all those who allowed us to share their stories, to our customers and the thousands of businesspeople with whom we have worked, partnered and competed over the years for providing us with the experience and knowledge contained herein.

We are eternally indebted to Leslie and Judith Fritz, Daryl Douglas and Margaret Mason, for all those things that parents do, and thankful that our other halves, Wiebke Benze and Oscar Lima, were willing to put up with 3.00 am calls and endless weekends of single parenting so that we had the time we needed to work on our little project.

And, of course, thank you to the patient waiters at Dee Bees Cafe who brought us an endless supply of coffee and courtesy as we debated the business of business.

Introduction

Dear Peter,

I'm writing to you on the first anniversary of your arrival in Australia. In celebration, you and your family are having a picnic.

You're lying on the grass in the dappled shade of the trees, listening to the chatter of other families and your own, which is underscored by the dry hum of the cicadas. This is the soundtrack to the overwhelming sense of freedom you've found in this new country. You still don't speak the language, but you know that will come. You've scrimped and saved with your parents to buy a small van — you don't need a showy car. You are 20 years old, and you're drunk on the sheer pleasure of living without the fear and paranoia that was so much a part of your life growing up in 1950s Romania.

Stop there. Stop what you're doing and slow down your thoughts. Savour the moment.

You have no meetings to attend, no obligations to fulfil, no network of friends or associates, no family to look after, and right now, no reason to rush. These will all come, but for the moment, just lie there and live in the now. Over the years you will gain strength from remembering that sense of absolute pleasure and peace and opportunity.

Your English will get better. You will make friends and you will go to university. You will work and study part time — and it will be worth it, so be prepared to persevere. Life is not lived in one great leap. It's made up of thousands of tiny steps, and you've still got a lot of walking to do. Take the time to finish what you start, and have the confidence to know that you are getting somewhere.

Don't be afraid of problems. You'll face many of them over the years, and you need to look on them as opportunities to develop your creativity. The problem will still be there tomorrow if you ignore it, and it will haunt you if you let it beat you. Face every challenge like a new opportunity and you'll make it through.

Don't be greedy. Greed is ugly and tasteless. We measure ourselves by externalities: titles, money, official recognition and so on. We calibrate ourselves to those around us and we will always find someone who is richer, smarter, more attractive and more successful. It takes a very strong person to break away from that, but if you spend your life looking over your shoulder, you will never be at peace with who you are and it will slow you down.

Obligations will come, and you'll fulfil them. At first they will feel overwhelming, and at times you will wonder how you're going to make it through. Trust yourself, pace yourself and don't choke.

Remember always that as humans we crave recognition and respect. Respect other people, not because of their achievements or possessions, but because your capacity to respect others is a powerful attribute which will serve you well. Make sure you provide those around you with that recognition and respect and they will repay you with the recognition and respect you will need to carry yourself through life.

There are only two decisions that will fundamentally change the course of your life. One was made for you when your parents brought you to Australia a year ago today. The other you'll make the day you realise that the company you are working for is about to close its doors. Just at that moment when everyone around you is preaching doom and gloom you will realise that you and some of your colleagues have the skills to keep the business going. But you will all struggle with the transition. You won't need bravery, intelligence or bravado. You won't need large amounts of capital. But you will need to undergo a fundamental shift in the way you view yourself. You will need to stop thinking like an employee, and begin to think and act like a business owner in your own right. The risk and responsibility will feel heady and disorienting, but you'll make it through, and soon enough you'll be too busy to think about it. Going into business for yourself will change everything. Embrace that change and don't be afraid of it.

By the time you reach my age, you will have spent a combined total of more than a year of your life on planes travelling back and forth to different business meetings. You will have worked alongside hundreds of people, from the cleaners you are working with now to the most powerful business leaders and politicians.

You will discover that success is not about what you achieve as an individual. Success is about finding and creating ideas that can grow into opportunities, services and products. Success for you will be about creating an entity called a business which will take on a life of its own, and grow and expand beyond your wildest dreams.

Don't run the race alone. Look for others and learn from them—run with them if you can. A team will always win against an individual player, and there is wisdom in a crowd, so listen to others but trust your own instincts for the final decision. And don't let anyone call you a workaholic—you'll enjoy doing what you do, so you'll never really need to work. Just follow the paths that engage your mind, and if it becomes all-consuming at times, go with it.

But right now coming to Australia has given you a moment of weightlessness. Your compass is spinning wildly as your life finds its direction again, and begins to point you to where you will go.

To paraphrase William Ernest Henley: you are the master of your fate and the captain of your soul.

Sincerest regards,
Peter Fritz
7 March 2010

Part I

The profit principle

Chapter 1

Introducing the profit principle

I'm not going to tease and taunt you and lead you on a journey of gradual revelation. There's no great secret you need to discover or bolt you need to unlock. There's no precious recipe or perfect formula that works every time.

What I'm going to give you upfront are the four key components of the profit principle.

You won't believe me anyway, so you'll need to read on to figure out exactly how to link what I've learnt through four decades of trial and error with your existing business or idea. But just so that you know from the very beginning: I've made a lot of mistakes, and the main reason

I'm writing this for you is so that you can sidestep those same errors. You're welcome to disregard what you read here and go ahead and commit those errors yourself—in fact, you probably will. But this way, at least you'll be off to a better start than I was when I peeled myself off that grass on that sunny afternoon a year after I arrived in Australia, because you won't be starting from zero.

The first and most fundamental part of the profit principle is that you don't need to spend money in order to make money. Yes, I know that's the opposite of what everyone's been telling you for years and years. The whole reason most people don't go out and start their own business is because they keep telling themselves that they need money to start a business. They believe that they need capital—they need to rent premises, print up cards and put up a website. In other words, they need to get and pay for all the trappings that will make them think they have a business.

... you don't need to spend money in order to make money.

But in reality, they have it backwards: you don't need to spend money to make money; you need to make money to make money. Business only works if there is more money coming into your company than is going out, yet we think we can't start a business without having money in the first place.

To implement this first part of the profit principle, you need to always opt for the solution that brings money into your business rather than the one that takes money out of your business. This is an approach you need to adopt from the very beginning. Don't hang up your shingle until you have a contract that will pay for the shingle to be made.

Don't print up cards until you have money coming in that will cover the costs of the printing.

It sounds crazy not because it is crazy, but because in order to understand this first principle you have to reject a lot of rubbish ideas you've been told (and probably repeated yourself for years and years).

Think about it for a minute. Having a pile of business cards and letterhead doesn't mean you are running a business—it means the local print shop is running a business. Having offices, desks, computers and printers doesn't mean you're running a business, it means the local office supply shop is running a business.

At this stage of the game, don't become what you seek; don't become a customer of other businesses before you find your own customers. To be successful, you must first find your own customers and use the money they pay you to print cards and make websites and organise all the trappings that make you think you have a company.

This brings me to the second part of the profit principle: your business isn't a business until you have customers, and it's not a successful business until using your goods and services becomes habitual to those customers.

Don't test your ideas out on friends and family—they will of course tell you that your ideas are great, because pumping up your ego doesn't cost them a cent. You'll soon discover that all this ego boosting is worthless compared to a single individual who happily hands over some cold, hard cash.

Your business will only be up and running when you can balance cash in and cash out, and if you're paying for the latest and greatest in e-commerce websites, printing business cards and renting office space before you've got your first customers, you've already failed.

So, how do you get a business started without a whopping capital investment? How do you promote your services without a print run of business cards? It's not as hard, or strange, as it sounds — it's just a matter of thinking a little more creatively than most people out there. Your point of difference will be that you can run your business in a cost-effective manner. Your profit will come when you understand how to make money before you spend money.

This brings me to the third part of the profit principle. Through years of experience I've discovered that the most straightforward way to start and run a business is to share both the risk and the responsibility by finding partners rather than doing or paying for everything yourself. Do what you know how to do and find partners to do the rest. Sweat equity, experience and corporate knowledge are all worth far more than any monetary value ever placed upon them, and the best way to increase the value of your business is to find partners with complementary skills and experience. Share the risk, share the profit and focus on expanding your human capital and skills base rather than going into debt.

Seeking partners rather than suppliers is also a great way to test out your business ideas. They can add experience and expertise, they bring along a complementary network of contacts, and they offer you a chance to spread your risk rather than shoulder it all yourself.

This partnership part of the profit principle can be extended to the way you find and treat staff as you grow, because the only way to get people to work effectively for you is if they understand the goals you are trying to achieve and have some kind of vested interest in doing their job well.

The fourth part of the profit principle is about what's going on in your own head. It's about understanding that you already have most of the skills you need to go into business for yourself. You already know what you need to know to start a business. You already have the skills, and someone is probably already paying you for them. The transition you need to make is from someone paying you for those skills as your employer, to someone paying you for those skills as your customer. That's the fundamental

You already know what you need to know to start a business.

difference between an employee and a businessperson or entrepreneur: employees depend on employers for their wages, while entrepreneurs and business owners depend on customers.

That's it, really — it's the core of all I've learnt over the past four decades, and while there are a lot of subtleties in the implementation, get these four points right and many of the other challenges will be much reduced.

Success in business is not rocket science. It's a matter of applying what you already know, ensuring that money comes in and not out, keeping your customers happy, and ensuring that your staff and partners are as keen to make your company succeed as you are.

Hold on to those ideas while you read on. The rest of the book will help to illustrate them with examples of people all around the world who've gone through the very same process of discovery. The transition from employee to employer is not easy, but it is interesting, it might be profitable, and it is certainly not what you expect. I know you can start your own business, and so do you. What we don't know is how exactly you'll be able to do it, given what you have and what you know. But the easy part comes right now, because all you need to do for the moment is to read on, to keep an open mind and to be just a little bit more curious.

Now that you have the four parts of the profit principle, I'm going to show you how to implement them through the examples of my own experiences, and those of other people. These people have all kinds of businesses, from fruit carving to telecommunications, mining and construction. Some of the businesses are very large, and some tiny. But they have all gone through similar phases of growth and similar challenges.

We'll look at why personal relationships are always crucial to the success of your business.

I'll begin by talking about how you start a business without going into debt, where your business comes from and how you can go about finding other people to work with (rather than buy from). It's about finding your place in the huge ecosystem of businesses of all sizes and shapes which every day buy and sell, thrive or wither, and do what it takes to ensure their own survival.

Then we'll look at how business is not done in a cold, impersonal climate. We'll look at why personal relationships are always crucial to the success of your business. Why trust between you, your staff, partners, suppliers and customers is fundamental to your success as an entrepreneur. Having found your place in this vast ecosystem of business, we'll look at how you hold onto your place by working with those around you.

Finally we'll look at growth. Once you've carved out a place in the business landscape, once you have established relationships with customers, staff and suppliers, how do you take this success and build on it? Do you spread the seeds of your own business across a broader landscape, or focus on putting down roots for a large single company?

You can pick your way through chapter by chapter, or dive in and out of the story at places that seem most relevant and interesting to you. Either way, there's much to discuss. So let's begin.

Chapter 2

Let's not start at the beginning

The first thing you need to learn—yes, even before you start your business—is that there is no beginning. There's no point in time where your business suddenly transitions from nothing to something, no matter how many certificates you have or what registrations you've managed to gather. The world isn't going to stop turning just so you can go into business, so you need to start looking for ways to slip in between what's already happening out there rather than waiting for your golden opportunity.

At some stage you'll register your company, secure a business number or lodge a tax return, but none of these processes actually prove you have a functional business. This is because businesses rarely have a discrete, recognisable beginning. They usually grow out of pre-existing businesses — they're a side operation that develops into its own market, a consultant who strikes out on their own with one or two key customers, or a technology that fails in one sector, but is picked up by another.

The beginning of one business is frequently sparked by the end of another. Often the most successful business-people have been to the brink of failure and back several times. TCG, now a multimillion-dollar group with businesses in fields as diverse as water management, technology development and business negotiation, is a great example. And it's an example I happen to know a lot about because it's the very first company I started. Now it acts as an umbrella group, sheltering and fostering new ideas and giving them the space and the infrastructure they need to grow and expand.

TCG was born out of the failure of a company called Mineral Securities that hit the rocks in the late 1960s. A mining boom driven more by stock market speculation than by ore deposits was coming to a sudden end, and Mineral Securities was caught up in the turmoil. But as is often the case, there were parts of the company that were still capable of functioning and making money.

Hidden away in a Sydney office tower were 26 propellerheads who ran the mineral technology consulting division called Scientific Computer Systems. Rather than accepting their fate, some of the technologists, myself among them, started looking for an alternative. We arranged to spin off a separate company, although it was immediately clear it would be impossible for a fledgling operation to sustain all 26 employees.

For the new operation to survive, it was vitally important that each participant would be able to convert their skills into earnings. Otherwise, the company would fail before it even started. The eventual consensus was that to participate in the new venture, each former Scientific Computer Systems employee would have to have at least three months of billable work ahead of them. These three months of work and guaranteed income would give the new venture the time it needed to get on its feet.

This was important for a number of reasons. In order to survive, the company had to be earning money. There was no investment capital to run with and no marketing fund to keep things going. To make the company fly, we would have to become business partners and do much more than research. We needed to be able to market our products and convince others to pay us for our services. Partnerships simply don't work unless everyone is able to contribute to the relationship, and they don't work unless everyone involved has a vested interest in making that contribution.

We needed to … convince others to pay us for our services.

Four researchers, including me, could fulfil these requirements, and so TCG was born. The notion of starting my own business with these colleagues was terrifying. I had worked hard to finish university part time, and I'd worked hard to get this job and to be taken seriously by businesspeople despite my accented English and my lack of connections in Australia. I'd done my best to win work for the company, and together with others in our small division, we'd been quite successful — but it was still a huge leap to change my mindset from that of an employee to that of an entrepreneur. But the choice was stark: the only way the business could continue to operate was if we took the risk of running it ourselves. It was that or the dole queue.

Although we didn't realise it at the time, in becoming entrepreneurs we former employees effectively started a business by doing what we were already doing. We simply began doing it for ourselves. Down the track 12 months, and we were still operational. In fact, we'd expanded the business and were earning more than we would ever have done as employees. That was all a long time ago, and the company has done extremely well, developed some very useful technologies, and made everyone involved rich in the process.

Businesses begin with a saleable skill and a single customer.

However, the question remains: if we were capable of running our own business, why hadn't we done so previously? Why did we allow others to profit from our skills, which were so clearly marketable? It was quite simply because when you're facing a challenging leap into a whole new experience, it's often easier to be pushed than to force yourself to jump. In fact, none of us might have made that initial transition unless we'd been pushed. We were comfortable and happy; we were working in challenging roles at a company that paid us well. The vertigo we felt looking down the precipice of having to find our own customers, balance our own pay sheets and turn this small division into a company in its own right was palpable.

A lot of very successful businesspeople became successful businesspeople because they found themselves in a position where they had no choice but to sell their skills directly to a customer, rather than relying on their employer to onsell their skills for a profit. A lot of people don't actually mean to go into business, but something comes along and pushes them. No neat beginnings and no business plans — just the sudden need to make their own money, and the often surprising discovery that people would pay them to do something they already know how to do.

Many successful companies begin without any real planning at all, let alone office space, letterhead and business cards. Businesses begin with a saleable skill and a single customer.

Gordon Merchant, founder of the Billabong brand, now has a fortune in the vicinity of $849 million. He began making and selling board shorts in 1973 to help pay for a house. He needed the money, had a skill and connected up the dots. And there are examples of this in every suburban shopping strip, and every local business directory in every country all over the world.

Suburban lawyer Alan Regal discovered something similar when he found himself unceremoniously sacked from his first 'real job' as a junior legal assistant in a law firm. Although he was expected to work long hours for terrible money, he'd taken the position because he felt he was too young and too inexperienced to start up on his own. The plan had been to work his way up through the firm for a few years, perhaps become a partner in a decade or so, and then begin to earn some real money.

Six months later, his job was terminated and he was faced with a difficult decision: either scratch around for another poorly paid position in a large firm, or try to hit out on his own.

Whether it's right or wrong, we are taught from a very young age to follow rather than to lead. We are taught to fall into step behind our parents, behind our teachers and later behind our bosses. The single most powerful force preventing most people from going into business for themselves is this *employee mindset* which is instilled in us from the time we come kicking into the world. All this training and indoctrination results in an insidious and almost irresistible urge to follow others rather than strike out on your own.

This is the reason most people spend years making their bosses rich, rather than going into business for themselves. You've probably done it yourself. In fact, you're probably doing it right now.

And certainly Regal, like you, wasn't even considering going into business for himself until he found himself unemployed. But as luck would have it, he picked up some work through word of mouth and, using this as a basis, went solo. Before he'd even had time to print up some business cards he had a list of clients and was rushing to register as a sole trader. His business took off, and within five years he'd achieved what would have taken him decades were he working for someone else.

As with many of us who work for other people, Alan didn't realise how many people he knew, and how much work could be generated simply by spreading the word among family and friends that you are open for business.

He had a very specific set of skills, but more importantly he had a big family and a broad group of friends who knew and trusted him, and it was from this group that he initially began establishing his customer base. Never underestimate the power of word of mouth, and the power your friends and family have to recommend you to others.

'But no!' I hear you cry. 'It isn't that simple! What about risk? What about business skills? What about profit and loss?'

And you're right: not everyone who finds themselves unexpectedly out of work is able to strike off on their own and immediately turn their misfortune into success. But what you have here is a whole book of examples of those who've done so successfully, as well as some examples of the failures, so that at the very least you've a chance to learn from others.

People don't fail in business because they are risk-averse. Good businesspeople are extremely risk-averse. Running a business isn't about taking risks, it's about avoiding risks. Some people secret away their extra cash to gather together the capital they think they will need to get started. Some mortgage their houses, or take out loans from banks or family. This is far riskier than not starting at the beginning!

... most people spend years making their bosses rich ...

Some people spend years planning the start of their business only to find themselves with piles of unused company stationery, an empty inbox and a company phone that never rings. Why do they fail? Because they start out with the assumption that business is all about risking your dreams and ideas and hard-earned cash on the off-chance that someone else will like your ideas enough to pay you for them.

They start at the beginning; they register a company name, hire an office and print up some stationery. They start by spending money, not by making it. They start by taking risks and expecting everyone else to behave in the way they've outlined in their business plans. Seasoned entrepreneurs know that they'll get further than that, and faster, by sitting down with a prospective customer and chatting about the product to gauge the reaction.

What you need to succeed in business is a customer...

What you need to succeed in business is more than an idea and more than an initial investment. What you need to succeed in business is a customer, and the best way to find and keep a customer is to start with a partner.

You already suspect you have the skills to go into business for yourself, or you wouldn't be reading this book. So let's start by figuring out what you know, what you do, and how to connect those skills with a customer.

Chapter 3

Your first product is you

If you don't already run your own company, stop reading for a moment and ask yourself: why not? Unless you're very lucky and have won the lottery or have some other way to perpetually support your needs, you probably already work—and you probably already work for someone else.

While it probably doesn't feel like it, this is a really good place to start because it means you have the basic skill required to survive in business: the capacity to do something that people will pay for. At the moment, whatever it is you're doing is being bought by your employer and sold on at a profit to a third person. If this weren't the case, the business you work for would be failing.

Take the example of Malcolm Crompton, who had spent several years working as Privacy Commissioner for the Australian federal government. As the use of biometric technologies, data warehousing and database analysis was becoming widespread in the commercial and government sectors, Crompton was advising the government as to what laws were needed to protect the public from the inappropriate use of personal information. He was good at his job, he had a thorough and comprehensive understanding of the issues associated with privacy and data use, and he was also coming to the end of his tenure as Privacy Commissioner.

Within a month we had ... our first customer.

Despite having other options, including a return to the public sector, Crompton was interested in finding a new challenge. He needed a role that would take advantage of the knowledge and skills he'd picked up in two decades of working for the government, but was not sure what that role would look like. He'd been a reformer, a lobbyist and a scientist, and as Privacy Commissioner he'd worked with competing requirements and complex legislation.

It was at this point I got involved. The company I'd founded decades earlier was still operating and had served as a launch pad for about a dozen other successful enterprises, and I could see that Crompton had a saleable skill. What he lacked was the commercial experience to turn those skills into an operational business.

I suggested we work together to create a privacy consultancy business. Rather than seek out an employer,

I suggested Crompton seek out customers who would pay him directly for his services. At first Crompton declined. He was looking for something more stable, including a stable income, and had not considered something that may not be so secure.

Being nothing if not tenacious, over several coffees and casual conversations I managed to convince Crompton that his skills were commercially saleable, and eventually we agreed to test the theory on the open market. Rather than register the business and print up cards and stationery, we would go out and, using our existing business contacts, seek a customer; someone who would pay Crompton directly for the skills he was attempting to sell via an employer.

Here's where the rubber hits the road: we both took the idea to market, offering data management consultancy to the government and the corporate sector. We trawled through our contacts lists, had meetings, shook hands and offered our services to everyone who would listen (and would be able to pay).

Within a month we had managed to sign up our first customer. Deloitte, then the world's second-largest professional services firm, was willing to pay Crompton a monthly retainer to do more or less what he had been doing for the federal government. A paying customer gave Crompton the money and the impetus to develop his skills into a brand, and Information Integrity Solutions (IIS) was formed.

Fast-forward 12 months and IIS had sold identity management and security consulting to companies including a number of banks, Cisco, IBM and Microsoft. What Malcolm didn't realise, and what many employees fail to realise until it's pointed out to them, is that his most valuable attributes were the contacts he'd built up over the years while working for others. He had accumulated a vast array of contacts in the corporate arena while working for the government. They'd worked with him in the past and they trusted his skills and knowledge in the privacy field. He understood the privacy ecosystem, he knew the businesses that were already established in this environment and knew what they needed to succeed.

What he didn't realise was that the same people he'd worked with in government were now willing to become his customers because they trusted him and knew he had the skills they needed. As a result Crompton was able to start his company with no brand, no stationery, no website, no telephone line other than his personal mobile phone and, most importantly, no money. Crompton's investment wasn't financial. It was intellectual and experiential, and he didn't follow his dream; he followed the skills he already had.

Your knowledge and skills are your main assets.

So, if you were to start a business, what would you do? What can you do? What do you know about? And more importantly still: what would people pay you to do?

Many small businesses fail early on because small business operators set out with the absurd assumption that people will pay them to fulfil their dreams, rather than catering to the needs and requirements of would-be customers.

If you want to fulfil your lifetime dream, do it on the weekend—but don't expect people to pay you for it. If you really want to succeed in business, figure out what people will pay you to do and hit the market. It's pointless, and heartbreaking, to spend your life dreaming of being your own boss if the work you want to do won't sell. Understanding this is the difference between being a skilled craftsperson and an entrepreneur. Both do something they enjoy, something they are good at, but a craftsperson focuses on the individual task at hand and does not see the wider picture of growing the business.

You can base your business around something you love, but you need to be prepared to work on the business itself. Start by asking yourself: what skills do you have? What skills are you already being paid for? It's a combination of these skills that could provide you with a clue as to where you could begin.

Your knowledge and skills are your main assets. All you need to figure out is how you can turn these into a saleable commodity, and who'll buy it from you when you do. Then it becomes a matter of finding those people.

So we've already established you have a saleable skill which is currently being sold for more than you're being paid. When you work within the bowels of a large corporation, the relationship between what you do every day and the profitability of the company isn't always obvious, but it's always there.

To understand your true economic value you need to figure out not just what you do, but what you enable others to do — that capacity to enhance the lives, enjoyment, well-being or productivity of others may well prove popular, as long as you can figure out how to sell it. If your skills enable other people to apply their skills to a profitable task, then people will pay you for your skills.

Of course when you're working for someone else they won't pay you the full value of your skills. But when you're working for yourself, the full value of whatever you sell comes back into your own business.

While it feels all safe and secure to be buried within another company, it's also easy to get lost and to be blinded to the connection between what you do and the profit someone else makes. Claiming that profit will require you to figure out how to turn what you already know into a business, and therein lies the true challenge of becoming your own boss.

Being a successful businessperson isn't about being able to do something better than anybody else, or even particularly well. It's about being able to sell what you know how to do.

Chapter 4

Start by making money, not spending it

Start by making money? I know you're sceptical, and so you should be. You probably read the business section of the newspaper, or follow who's investing in what via online business forums. You've heard all about venture capital and angel investment, but what you really need to understand is that newspapers and magazine stories are about companies that are already operating. The directors and owners of these companies have already established that they can make money from their skills, or that they can sell their products and services for a profit.

In 1964, at just 18 years of age, Solomon Lew took over the running of what was then a small clothing business his father had founded before his death when Solomon was just 13. Like most small businesses, the company was a way for the family to survive. Prosperity came much later as Solomon expanded into textiles and toys, real estate and retail.

Now one of Australia's richest businessmen, with a line of retail brands and an estimated personal wealth just a tad over $1 billion, Lew began as his own employer and built his corporate empire with sweat equity. The millions of dollars he spends on his business have already been generated by that business, or are raised based on the fact that his business is already turning over billions of dollars in revenue each year. And he's not the only one.

After years of babysitting, selling lemonade and part-time jobs at Coles, Carolyn Creswell took all the money she had ($1000) and became her own boss by buying the company where she'd been working: Carman's Fine Foods. In that first year she mixed the muesli by hand and sold a little over 80 kilograms of her wares. She now sells more than 40 tons of oats, fruit and nuts in her muesli bars and cereal mixes a year, to 22 countries all over the world. But the leap wasn't immediate. It took 16 years and a lot of hard work to create a company with $16 million in revenue.

... these people ... began with no credit, no credit rating and no significant capital investment.

What these people have in common is that they began with no credit, no credit rating and no significant capital investment. They began by selling and worked their way up by reinvesting in their business, using one revenue stream to lead to the next. At every stage they remained actively engaged in selling what they did. This is the key to the success of just about any business you care to name.

So, we've established that you already have a set of skills that are marketable, you're selling them to your employer, and they are bundling those skills up with other elements to make a saleable (and profitable) product or service.

So why doesn't everyone give up working for others and set up on their own? Mostly because they think that starting a business will require large amounts of capital or debt. But most people are wrong. Starting a business requires large amounts of energy, a particular skill that is saleable and the ability to get out there and sell whatever that skill happens to be. It does not require startup money.

Most people assume that the most important investment you make in your business is liquid capital: money. And rather than getting out there and looking for a way to begin their company, they scrimp and save, or worse, go into debt, in order to get things started.

In all business cash flow is king, but credit and capital can poison even the most promising business before it even gets off the ground. Why?

Well, the biggest danger of starting a business with a large amount of cash is that it will begin to function in a totally unrealistic way. Rather than set out to make money, the first thing you'll do is spend like crazy on letterheads, websites, and business cards.

It all feels great because it's much more comfortable to spend money than it is to make money. It's always easier to be a buyer than a seller. In reality, you may as well simply donate your hard-earned cash to other businesses. None of this is of any use until you know where your customers will come from.

As long as you don't throw all your money away early by starting out in an unsustainable spending spree, you'll have the opportunity to try a couple of different markets and a couple of different approaches. Sometimes ideas take some time to develop a market, which is why setting up your business in a sustainable way, with minimal overheads, is the best way to ensure you'll make it through the initial phase of market development.

You don't need money to make money; you need customers to make money.

Most small businesses go to the wall in the first 12 months because, rather than finding a customer, they focus on setting up their infrastructure. What they fail to realise is this: websites are useless unless you have customers who want to visit them, letterhead is useless unless you have someone to invoice and office space is useless until you have a stream of paying customers to meet.

You don't need money to make money; you need customers to make money.

And you don't need money to get customers; you need a product, skill or service for which customers are willing to pay. Your role as a small-business operator is to connect all this together; figure out what people want, and how to give it to them for a price they're willing to pay.

Chapter 5

The customer doesn't owe you their business

Okay, so far we've dealt with the myth that companies begin with some kind of discrete, easily recognisable beginning, and that you need money to make money. But here is one truism that is not a myth: all companies need customers. An idea or dream is a necessary but insufficient starting point for any business, because until you can find a customer willing to pay for that dream, you have no business.

Business is driven not by ideas, and not by start-up finance, but by selling a skill to paying customers. From the vast fast-food empire of McDonald's down to your local hamburger bar, none of these businesses survive unless customers walk through the door and pay for a meal. IIS didn't get started because we had capital and dreams, but because we had skills and a customer.

So what is a customer, and how do you get one? More importantly, how do you get one who will pay you for *your* services?

As it turns out, the word *customer* in English is derived from *custom*—or habit. A custom is an act that, for whatever reason, is regularly repeated within a culture or social group. A customer is a person who regularly goes somewhere and does, buys, eats or watches something repeatedly. Repetition is important. Repetition is what is going to get you not only your initial income, but repeat sales. And once they've walked across your threshold the first time, the most important thing you need to do is to ensure that they come back.

If someone walks into your coffee shop and buys a coffee then walks out feeling sold to, but not satisfied, and never returns again, you'll only make $1 from their trade. If they walk out with a coffee and a smile, having been greeted with a friendly face and pleasant conversation, they'll be good at least for a follow-up coffee, if not a lunch booking.

It was this discovery that enabled the Sammut family to revolutionise the nursery industry in Australia through the establishment of the Flower Power chain of nursery stores. In the 1970s, plant nurseries were small-scale family-run businesses. They were invariably cramped and damp, a design that was great for plant growth, but not very customer-friendly.

Beginning with a small nursery, the Sammuts separated the sales area from the greenhouse where the plants were grown, then levelled and paved it. They made it easy to walk in between the rows of plants, supplied trolleys and extended the range of garden-related goods they sold.

They would go on to launch one of the first customer loyalty programs ever, supplying customers with magazines about gardening, vouchers to encourage return sales and, finally, cafés and play areas to ensure the shopping experience was pleasant, all of which encouraged customers to come back.

The success of the Flower Power nurseries is not down to their large range of healthy garden plants—there are several hundred small, successful plant nurseries around Australia that offer just that. What the Sammuts provide their customers at their nurseries with are great plants and a great shopping experience, all in a pleasant environment that's well stocked, easy to access and with a coffee thrown in for good measure.

When a customer walks through your door, they walk into a new experience.

When a customer walks through your door, they walk into a new experience. It matters little or not at all if they buy something on that initial visit, as long as they return—as long as dealing with your business becomes their custom.

The same goes for any business transaction. The purpose of the first meeting isn't to sell anything. The purpose of the first meeting is to ensure a second meeting occurs. If you happen to sell something at the same time, then it's an added benefit—but a sale shouldn't be the goal. Give your customers the time and space to feel comfortable in dealing with you, and make it in their interest to return. This is as true for your corner store as it is for your computer distribution business or your waste management service.

The most important thing about customers is that they are prepared to give you money in exchange for something you know how to do, or for a product you know how to make. But you can't *expect* them to do anything at all. Zip, zero, nothing, nada, zilch; the customer doesn't owe you their business—you owe them yours!

Self-interest is the only reason they'll come anywhere near you, and it's the best incentive to encourage their repeated custom. Your job is to make them want to walk back through your doors sometime soon—and, even better, recommend you to a friend.

In fact, the mistake many would-be businesspeople make is to focus on what they can *do*, and forget to pay attention to whether or not they can sell what they do. The closer you are to this coalface of interaction with the customer, the more difficult it is to do business. It's easier and vastly more interesting to research a new technology than it is to develop it into a saleable product. In turn, product development is easier and more interesting than actually selling the final product. Invoicing someone else's sales and balancing the books in someone else's company is easier, and feels a heck of a lot safer, than balancing your own.

... the customer doesn't owe you their business—you owe them yours!

This is why most of us are quite content to simply amble into someone else's company, get a salary and never sell a bean. But while selling is hard, it's not impossible, and there are techniques that make it a bit easier.

The first hurdle you need to overcome is the idea that other people will want to buy something just because you want to sell it. Having your heart set on selling a particular good or service to the exclusion of all others is a great way to not succeed in business, and it's a really bad way to start out. For starters, your customers have no reason to like what you like, and no interest in spending money on things that you think they should buy.

Starting a business is not a way to fulfil your dreams; it is a way to make a living. In fact, starting out in business to fulfil your dreams is a great way to destroy both your dreams and your income.

In order to succeed in business, you need to sell what customers want — not what you want — or there's simply no point in starting out.

It would be wonderful if everybody could simply set up a business and earn a living based on their favourite pastime, but that's not the way it works. You need to sell what people will buy. People might want to buy what you want to sell — if you're lucky they will — but before you start out, it's a good idea to test the market. Put it out there and see how people react.

Having worked for others for years in uninspiring roles, Andrew Chavez quit his job and set himself up as a translator. He had all the right qualifications, had worked in the field overseas, and was desperate to find a job that was more rewarding than the clerical role from which he'd resigned. He set up a home office, printed up cards, applied for a business number and changed his answering message.

But the phone didn't ring. And when it finally did, he was so desperate for the work he cut his prices back to the point where he may as well have been living on welfare. After years of dreaming of running his own business, he spent six months running up his credit card debt before he began to apply again for paid work.

It was a horrible, harrowing experience. There was nothing wrong with Andrew's skills as a translator—he knew his craft well—but he didn't know how to win business as a translator. Running a business is about more than performing a task. Running a business is about finding people to pay you to perform a task.

If people find your proposition interesting they will feed you and pay your mortgage. If they find it particularly interesting they may even get together and spend enough money on your goods and services to let you go out and buy a yacht.

If they don't like it, don't give up hope! You may be focusing on the wrong market, or packaging and pricing yourself in the wrong way, and we'll deal with all of that later.

In a weird kind of way your first customer may well be your business partner—it may be a government organisation that agrees to give you money to turn your idea into a company.

The main thing to remember about customers is that you need to find a way to integrate your products or services into their everyday lives. You need to make using your services or products part of their habitual activities. Make it easy and pleasant for them so they'll come back again and again.

Many unsuccessful businesses fail because they focus on winning customers rather than keeping customers. They spend millions on marketing, then fail to offer an experience that lives up to the expectations they've encouraged. Finding customers costs you time, money and effort so once you've managed to convince them to walk through the door, it's worth your while ensuring they get what they need. Even very large companies often make this mistake, creating fantastic deals or price reductions for new customers, while rarely offering their existing customers any incentive to stay. Think of the telecommunications company that offers new connections at half the rate their existing customers pay. Sure, it creates an incentive for new customers to join, but it also creates an incentive for existing customers to seek better service elsewhere.

> *If people find your proposition interesting they will feed you and pay your mortgage.*

Companies that are so desperate to find new customers that they neglect their existing customers will ultimately fail. While gaining a customer is costly, losing one is even more costly.

People are creatures of habit. We like doing things we've done before, so once you've convinced them to come over to your side, most of your customers will prefer to stay with you. People also like to boast about how clever they are at discovering this or that product or service; we like to talk about what we buy and the services we use with other people because we think it makes us look smart.

A single happy customer is worth thousands of dollars in terms of advertising, while a single unhappy customer will cost you tens of thousands of dollars to win back.

So why is it that so many companies focus more on winning new customers than on keeping existing customers happy? Mostly because business operators fail to understand some of the basic principles of accounting. They measure and reward new customer acquisition, rather than measuring and rewarding happy customer maintenance.

Structure your business around not just winning customers, but around keeping them, and keeping them on-side. Then you'll manage to ensure that holy grail of business: the ongoing revenue stream.

No customer at any stage owes you their business, even if they came by yesterday, even if they were shopping with you a week before, even if they've been with you for a decade or more. Your job is to give them a reason and incentive to come back, many times over.

If you've been to any small business course worth its salt, you will have been shown how to write a business plan. While it's an interesting exercise in imaginative planning, it's not a very good way to determine how the big wide world is going to respond to your ideas.

Here's a little secret they didn't tell you when they were showing you how to write that business plan: customers don't read them.

That's right. There it is, all out in the open. Your customers, potential or existing, have no idea what you are expecting of them, and that's the way it should be. Even if they had read your plans, they're under no obligation to respond to them in the way you want them to, no matter how clearly you set it out.

The problem with business plans is that they dictate how the world will need to behave in order for your idea to work. But the world of customers out there has no reason to behave according to what you've written down. For better or worse for your business, customers will behave in a way that is entirely rational, and probably far more sensible than anything you're capable of thinking up.

That's just the way these things work. No-one likes being told what to do, and when you're trying to get someone to turn up regularly and give you their money, you shouldn't start out by burdening them with all your assumptions. That's why your business isn't a business until you've tested your product in the real world. Your business isn't a business until you have a customer.

In the meantime, pull out that business plan you've got tucked away and give it an overhaul. Whether it's written down, in your head or merely the speck of an idea that's been bugging you for a while, ask yourself this: does it allow you to get the business going *No customer at any stage owes you their business...* without risking your own money, or leaving your current role? Does it require you to spend vast amounts of money before securing your first deal? Can it be reworked to focus entirely on securing a customer in the initial phase?

Keep thinking and read on, because while securing a customer is one absolutely fundamental step towards beginning your own business, there are other areas you'll also need to consider.

Chapter 6

Fishbones are small, but you can choke on them

It's often hard to understand exactly what entrepreneurs do. If you glance through the country's leading business publications you'll find these people have an incredible range of backgrounds. Some have university degrees, some barely finished high school, some have spent a lot of time working in one sector and others have careers that span a range of different areas.

Malcolm Turnbull is a classic example of a business-person whose principal focus is on, well, business. Legally trained, he's worked as a banker, a broker, an investor, a journalist, a politician and, oddly enough, even a lawyer.

He has been a managing director, he manages real estate, owns cattle and, in the decade from 1999 to 2009, managed to increase his personal fortune from $65 million to $178 million.

While Turnbull understands the intricacies of the businesses that he's been involved with over the years, his principal talent lies in getting stuff done by finding other talented individuals to do it for him.

Running your own business means you'll need to take responsibility for IT systems, printing, accounting, invoicing, banking, tax, marketing and advertising, warehousing, inventory, production, suppliers, inputs, waste management and so on and so forth. You are responsible for it—but you don't necessarily have to do it all, all the time.

What about all that other stuff about which you know nothing? How on earth do you track your profits and losses? How do you ask people for money? How do you figure out your pricing? What should you pay for company premises? Where do you put your offices?

Whoa, stop right there. You're trying to end up with a company, not a coronary. All this stuff can look really scary from the outside, and really scary if you've never done it before. Unfortunately this is where a lot of people get stuck.

The employee mindset, the pull of making other people rich by sitting happily within someone else's corporate structure, is extremely powerful. One of the reasons it is so powerful is that it lets you do what you know you can do, and lets other people worry about the details that you don't know about.

Here's the big secret that no-one tells you because they don't want you out there on your own, competing with them. Quick—glance around to check that no-one is reading over your shoulder.

Coast clear?

Okay…here goes…

It's not that hard.

If accounting were really difficult we'd say things like 'After all, it's not accounting…' to describe things that are really easy. No-one says that. People compare hard things with rocket science and easy things with a walk in the park. And, okay, accounting isn't quite a walk in the park, but accountants aren't revered as hyper-smart pinheads with Coke-bottle glasses either. It's not all that hard to do, it's just a matter of learning the processes—and you can do that at just about any community college or weekend course.

Here's the big secret that no-one tells you…

Like Turnbull, you need to know how to get the ball rolling, but if you imprison yourself in the back room doing the books, you won't be able to get out onto the streets to actually sell the business. As an entrepreneur you always need to be on hand to sell the company and its products, not fiddling around with administrative tasks. Ask around and find a decent small business accountant, get them to recommend some software and there you have it. Done and dusted.

You'll need to register your company, organise insurance, find premises and figure out how to track what's coming in and what's going out. This isn't what you do; this is what you need to do in order to do what you do.

Don't be intimidated; these are simply processes. They've been done a trillion times before and you don't need to figure any of them out from scratch. There are easy ways to learn them and, if not, there are easy ways to get someone else to do them for you.

Like fishbones, you need to know this administrative stuff is around, and you need to know more or less how to manage your way through it, but you can't let it choke you. Fear of administration is often what prevents people from ever profiting from their own skills, and it's just about the silliest excuse you'll find. When you're a small business owner you need to do everything yourself, and this can be both challenging and daunting.

Don't be intimidated; these are simply processes.

When I first started my own company I can remember feeling overawed by the amount of red tape and compliance we needed to fulfil simply to go on and sell our wares, but I soon discovered that most of these processes are repetitive and really quite easy. Almost invariably there's a course you can do or a government department there to explain the details, so don't be afraid to ask around to find out how other people get their own work done. Don't spend years wondering how you will learn to run a business. Find someone who already knows how and convince them to go into partnership with you, or go out there and start it and learn by doing.

After years of working for other people, Nene and Darryl Brown wanted to go into business for themselves. A master painter by trade, Darryl Brown had spent a quarter of a century making other people's businesses successful. He knew his trade, and while that was earning him enough to live on, he was happy enough to go with the flow. Besides, fiddling around with the paperwork wasn't his forte.

But there was one thing he wanted to do but couldn't while he was working for other people. Being of Aboriginal origin, he wanted to create real work opportunities for Indigenous kids. Together with his wife Nene, Darryl attended a small business course at a local community college and within a matter of weeks picked up the basic knowledge he needed to get a business off the ground. Yet 12 months later, his business, Ability Plus, was doing poorly and very nearly went to the wall.

Working as a partnership, Darryl and Nene seemed totally unable to win big tenders and were trying to make ends meet with small contracts. In charge of the office side of things, Nene did some research and discovered that operating as a partnership rather than a business precluded them from big contracts. Within a month they re-registered as a business, sold the old partnership to themselves and finally they had the paperwork they needed to win the big deals.

From then on they started winning some big tenders and growing rapidly. Another 12 months down the track and Ability Plus had become a very successful company with 10 staff, three full-time Indigenous apprentices and plans to recruit a further seven apprentices later in the year.

So while a lot of the information you need to run a company is readily available through short courses, sometimes you need to get inside an industry before you get access to the insider information that you need to know.

So do what you know, get out there and sell the business and don't choke on the small stuff.

Chapter 7

How to remember something you never knew

There is a lot of talk about business intuition—the ability of an entrepreneur to act on gut instinct and respond quickly to a challenge, almost without thinking. But don't be conned into thinking that there's anything spiritual or otherworldly about what they're doing. Successful entrepreneurs have spent years learning and internalising the ability to quickly see the most cost-effective and strategic approach to solve a problem.

This ability to rapidly make decisions is something that often comes naturally to people who have spent a lot of time working within a particular sector, or who have grown up in an entrepreneurial family.

Take, for example, Anthony Pratt, who became the head of the Visy empire following the death of his father, Richard Pratt. In assuming the Visy throne, Pratt junior became Australia's richest man with a personal fortune estimated to be in the vicinity of $5.48 billion.

However, inheriting vast personal wealth is no guarantee of success. James Packer, within four years of his father's death, had managed to lose more than half the $3 billion he'd inherited, due largely to a fall in the value of the family's investments because of the global financial crisis.

With an estimated fortune of $3.4 billion, Gina Rinehart is far and away Australia's richest woman. She'd grown up working with her father in the family *... inheriting vast* business, and had the privilege of *personal wealth is no* seeing it from the inside from a very *guarantee of success.* young age. But she did not inherit her wealth; it was earned because she had the vision and the work ethic to breathe new life into what was a moribund, debt-ridden company. She paid off the company's debts and learnt to work with other companies to share the cost and the risk of new projects. Iron ore projects that her father had tried to develop for almost four decades are now operational, thanks to partnerships with BHP Billiton. Partnerships allow her to share the risk, and give her access to a tremendous base of human resources and intellectual capital that she would have had difficulty attracting or maintaining during a mining boom.

What all these individuals have had is the experience and knowledge built up through exposure to their families' business dealings. Men like Pratt and Packer, and women like Gina Rinehart, have grown up talking business from a very young age. They've had the opportunity to mix and speak with highly skilled individuals, and the opportunity to understand what lies at the heart of profitability within their parents' businesses. This kind of experience is invaluable and will be crucial to the ongoing financial success of their families.

But for the rest of us, this entrepreneurial instinct is something we need to learn. My own family had a series of small businesses, which taught me a little about what to do, and a lot about what not to do, when I finally took charge of my own.

The value of big companies such as Visy and Publishing and Broadcasting Limited is not merely represented through the assets they hold. The real value comes in the form of the massive wealth of business knowledge such organisations hold within. The leader's role is to foster and develop this talent because without it the company has no future. These companies have what we'll call *corporate memory*; they know how to keep the engine running so that the car will be able to go places.

Corporate memory is extremely valuable. It's what makes it possible to create infrastructure, set up procedures and adopt work patterns that ensure that each person within the company is able to focus on what they do best. It's what makes large companies so efficient at monitoring income and paying bills and wages.

The challenge when you're first setting out in business is that you have very little corporate memory on which to base your own procedures and processes. While this can seem totally overwhelming, the most important thing to remember is that most of these processes already exist. So if you don't know how to do something, go and ask someone.

Even if you have never run your own business, you already apply a lot of these skills in running your home. Every week, you balance income with expenditure, get bills paid, groceries bought and cooking and cleaning done.

Taking the same approach to your business is often quite simple, but when you're employed by someone else you're only exposed to a small proportion of the administrative side and forced to focus on whatever it is you're being paid to do. You can lose confidence in your capacity to actually run your own company. That lack of confidence will leave you forever imprisoned in the employee mindset, and forever making money for others rather than for yourself.

The great news is that you don't need to reinvent any of these processes in order to run your own successful venture. In fact, the best way to go about gaining corporate memory is to copy someone else.

The important thing to remember is that none of the administrative side of things is core to your business: you and your skills are at the core, so don't let any of this stuff get in the way. Much of it can be simplified or automated using readily available software packages. In fact, finding a good IT business support service can be as critical to your ongoing success as finding a good accountant.

Another shortcut to finding out what you need to know is becoming a franchisee. Franchisees literally buy corporate memory and brand recognition from the franchisor, which is why they tend to be vastly more successful than stand-alone businesses, especially in the first couple of years of operation.

Audrey Mason wanted to cast off the employee mindset and join the 1.2 million other Australians who have left paid employment in favour of the thrill of owning and managing their own company.

On the surface, Mason's prospects didn't seem all that good. She had no small business experience, nor did anyone in her family. She lacked the upfront capital to buy into an established enterprise, had never seen a profit and loss sheet and knew next to nothing about human resources or staff management. With the small business failure rate hovering around 50 per cent, she began to look for ways to mitigate that risk while still fulfilling the dream of becoming her own boss. Five years later, she owns

... the best way to go about gaining corporate memory is to copy someone else.

three coffee shops, manages nearly 70 staff members, and handles everything from the cappuccino machine to staff recruitment—even those dreaded profit and loss sheets.

But at the outset, things didn't look so good. Her saleable skills were all intangible personal attributes: she was good with people and had a lot of energy. How do you turn hyperactive happiness into cold, hard cash? Mason's answer was to buy the business smarts and the corporate memory from a café franchise, use her interpersonal skills to recruit and motivate staff, and create a base of regular customers. Although it might look like it, she's not making money out of selling coffee; she's making money by using her people skills to run a series of cafés.

And franchising isn't the only means of gaining corporate memory. Once you know what you don't know, getting your business started might just come down to finding someone who's been there before. Starting your own business can feel a bit like jumping off a cliff: it takes a heck of a lot of courage. If you can't make the jump alone, finding someone else to jump with is a seriously good idea.

Another way to enhance your corporate memory is to seek out business partners who can share your vision, complement your skills and provide extra motivation. What you need is to find someone who knows what you don't, so you can pool your resources and together gain the corporate memory you lack when operating alone.

If you need to call upon the skills of others to keep the business going, look for ways to include them in the long-term success of the company rather than simply offering them a short-term profit. Sure, it may mean you have to forgo a small proportion of your revenues, but it's a neat way of spreading risk.

Why not ask the shopfitter to forgo his short-term profit of $10 000 for a proportion of the company's longer term profits? Why pay the consultant *What you need is to find someone who knows what you don't...* who writes up your tender documents a salary, when she might find it more interesting to be remunerated based on a percentage of overall government grants received? Why not gather together a group of hairdressers who each invest in their own infrastructure within the hairdressing salon, and then share the profits commensurably?

There are always ways to get the knowledge and resources you need, while also sharing the risks and benefits of business. It's just a matter of shifting your thinking. In fact, some of the most successful businesspeople are not the people who have the skills they need to succeed in business, but those who can recognise such skills in others.

Sometimes it comes down to aligning yourself with people who are already successful. Seek them out, pitch your idea, and offer to marry what you know with what they know. Make your potential partner your first customer, because if they are already making money, chances are they will recognise a good business idea when they see it.

But don't get too upset if your idea doesn't really excite them. In fact, just keep looking and pitching until you find someone who will take you seriously. If you're smart, you'll use each failed pitch to learn something new and to tweak and modify your proposal.

When looking for a partner, remember you are looking to go into a relationship with someone. You need to find someone who suits your temperament, complements your skills and is easy for you to get along with. You need to find someone with whom you can disagree, and disagree strongly, but not take it personally. Take your time, get to know them, progress from an idea to a contract where each party agrees to how they are going to contribute to the company, and how you will jointly move into the first phase.

Usually this means outlining the skills and expertise you are each going to bring to finding that first customer who will make your company a reality. You have a partner, then you have a customer, then you have a cash flow and only *then* do you actually have a business.

Chapter 8

Curiosity is the key

You're probably realising by now that it is indeed possible to begin your own business, knowing what you already know and doing what you already do. As long as you don't spend any money until you make money, you'll be most of the way to actually having a successful business. You might still want to go off to complete this course or get that certificate, but ultimately the best way to learn how to run a business isn't by reading and learning about other businesses, it's about getting out there and doing it yourself.

Statistics are great if you want a bird's eye view of what's going on in the world, but no business is a statistic, and statistics won't be able to tell you how to behave. In fact, they can provide you with a very warped view of what is actually going on. Global averages suggest every family on earth has precisely 2.6 children. A good example of the misleading nature of averages is that a booming economy can bring poverty to one sector while endlessly enriching another, a fact that is never properly reflected in the gross national product. Governments, researchers and universities all rely on statistics to get some kind of overarching view of what is going on in the economy, but there's no reason you should feel in any way obliged to reflect or follow the statistics on which these groups rely.

Your business is not a statistic. It is as individual as you are, and your relationships in business depend not on the surrounding statistics, but on your own capacity to earn and learn. Learning in business is something that begins from the first time you utter the phrase

... curiosity is one of the most powerful forces for success.

'I have an idea...', and runs through every handshake, order, invoice, advertisement, contract and agreement you make. You can read lots of books and attend lots of courses, but ultimately the only way you'll fully understand your business and how it will interact with the rest of the economy is to go out there and test your ideas.

So what is it that drives you? What is it that will make you get up tomorrow, pick up the phone and begin to work on your business idea?

Greed works for some. The desire to have money and the power and prestige it brings is certainly a powerful driver for many. But greed fails in terms of motives because it makes money and power, rather than success, the end game, and this can lead to short-sightedness in terms of the way you manage your company and your relationships.

In business and in life, curiosity is one of the most powerful forces for success. Curiosity trumps greed when it comes to business, mostly because greed is a passion that pushes you to become wealthier than those around you, while curiosity drives you to understand their success and look for ways to emulate it, or to come at it with a different approach.

Smart salespeople attend the workshops of visiting sales gurus not to learn their techniques, but to learn what not to do with a customer, so that their pitch does not come across as old and clichéd. Their curiosity leads to observation but not emulation, an important approach for many.

Courses, certificates and degrees are useful because they provide you with all the details in an easy-to-read, easy-to-reach format, but they are no replacement for direct experience, in the same way that an online directory or telephone book is no replacement for a little black book of contacts you actually know and trust.

This is where your success in business will always come back to you and your capacity to take in vast tracts of information, statistics, research, courses and theories, and select those that best fit your particular situation. Business does not take place between sets of statistics, but between groups of people. It's as personal as it is professional — you need to look people in the eye and figure out whether you can trust them and get them to trust you, none of which can be taught though a textbook or a course.

The best way to assess a business idea is to ask other businesspeople, not consultants, academics or analysts, but real on-the-ground businesspeople; the people you would sell to or buy from, the people you would partner with or work against as a competitor.

This is why curiosity is a more powerful motivation than greed. Greed will tell you to add up the figures once or twice, set in motion an operation and follow it through to its logical conclusion. Curiosity will force you to be forever asking, 'what if...' and 'how come...', and all the other open-ended questions that lead creative people down paths that others either ignore or fail to notice.

In my own case, curiosity was a basic survival skill as a young man in a new country. Without it, I would never have understood the culture of this new place. Everything around me was new and different, and the only way to move forward was to constantly ask myself, 'why?' and 'how?', as there was no longer any status quo to accept. I carried this into business, and it has in turn carried me into a whole range of new business opportunities. Curiosity is also crucially important in negotiation, but I'll talk more about that in later chapters.

You are not a statistic, and neither are [your customers].

Curiosity will force you to constantly assess and reassess what you are doing and whether or not you are taking the best approach. Constant, honest self-assessment is the only way to get some sense of how you affect those around you. This is crucial in leadership, because a true leader needs the capacity to convince those around them to do what they want them to do. Curiosity will enable you to compete and cooperate all at the same time, and sometimes with the same people at the same time, which is an incredibly powerful approach if you manage to pull it off.

Curiosity will force you to constantly ask what your customer wants and needs. It will force you to go out and talk to them, rather than sitting back and assuming you know what they want based on numbers measured, collated and analysed by others. You are not a statistic, and neither are they.

Innovation is not something you should do with religious fervour after paying someone else to do the research. Innovation is something you should do every day, as a matter of course, because it's good to change the status quo. Changing the status quo is dangerous but necessary, because businesses that aren't able to change are doomed to become trapped when the ground suddenly moves from underneath them.

Curiosity will help you to see these changes ahead of time; it will allow you to think through the different scenarios that will help you to change and modify your business according to the changing landscape. Curiosity will make you resilient and strong in the face of adversity and diversity.

Curiosity will force you to look out for yourself, and look out for your customers, but most importantly curiosity will force you to look for the most original way around a problem. It will force you to find the resolution that provides the best outcome for everyone involved.

Curiosity will ensure that you and your business will never be generalised out of existence. Your customers will always find you responding to their needs and their desire to get the most result for the least effort. Ultimately, curiosity, and not greed, will ensure your business is a success now and for as long into the future as you are able to see and respond to adversity.

So next time someone comes to you with numbers, refuse to be counted in. By counting yourself out, you may just achieve far more than you ever would as another simple statistic.

Chapter 9

The myth of perpetual motion

Finding your first customer is great, because it means that you have a business and that there is at least one person who'll pay you for what you know how to do. The first customer is necessary to your business, but they are not sufficient to keep your business operating. You can't depend on perpetual motion to ensure your business keeps moving; you actually need to keep on pushing so that it doesn't stop. Your first customer is important, but only insofar as they enable you to stay in business for your next customer, and from that one to the next one, and so forth. Nothing moves, at least not in the way that you want it to, unless it is being pushed. The main challenge in going from one customer to many is that you need to learn how to juggle the twin demands of finding and fulfilling contracts at the same time.

Often the issue for small businesses is that they are usually started by someone with a specific skill set, and it's often a skill set that has nothing to do with the actual running of a business. The mere fact that you've spent money on this book probably indicates you have a skill set you believe others will pay for, and you're probably right. But to run your own business you don't just have to be good at what you already do; you'll also need to gain skills that deal with growing and tracking your customer base.

See, starting your own business isn't just about what you know how to do; it's also about getting others to pay you for it. And that means finding a way to market yourself and your trade. Take Richard Jenkins as a case in point. A qualified carpenter, Jenkins was working for a large construction firm when he offered to help a friend put together a kit cubby house one weekend. The work was easy, the result rewarding and, after a few back-of-the-envelope calculations, he figured out he could make more money building two or three cubby houses per week than he did in his current position.

Excited about the prospect of being his own boss, he hit the phone, called a few businesses, and eventually came up with a couple of different business models. One was to work with a couple of his own designs, either supplying the cut timber as kits, or offering to provide a complete build for an extra fee. At the very least he would make a retail margin on the cut timber, and at best he would also pick up a payment for the construction work.

But then the whole idea hit a little snag. A skilled carpenter, Jenkins knew nothing about marketing. With a mortgage to pay he wouldn't be able to risk giving up his day job unless he already had a series of jobs lined up. The cost of advertising in the local paper was prohibitive and he had no idea how to go about actually finding customers in the first place. What he needed was a way to find his first couple of customers, and to line up a series of jobs before he left his current employment. Rather than leap into the unknown, he took some extra time to look at the cubby house market.

... starting your own business isn't just about what you know how to do ...

There were a number of cubby house franchises on offer around the country, and not only did they offer access to prepackaged designs and supplies, they also offered tips and techniques when it came to marketing. However, buying into such a franchise also required a substantial initial investment.

Seemingly trapped between a number of options that required initial capital he simply did not have, he then discovered that the cubby he had first built had been bought on an online auction site. Then things began to move more quickly. Web-based advertising was vastly less expensive than print alternatives. He made up a picture based on one of his own cubby designs and posted it on the website. To be safe, he posted the price as the minimum fee, and provided a separate fee to actually deliver the timber and build the house. Within a week he'd found a customer, built a cubby and sent his first invoice.

So he posted another cubby on the auction site, but this one didn't sell. He tried again, and got a sale. It took a couple of months and a few mistakes for Jenkins to figure out how best to use the auction site but, because it was so cheap to list goods for auction, he could afford to make a few mistakes.

His trick was to never spend more than he made. Not every ad resulted in a sale, but his advertising budget was only ever taken out of money he already had in the bank, so there was no danger of him spending more than he could earn.

Finally, he had a breakthrough. Someone called him and asked for a quote. By this stage he'd installed about half a dozen cubbies and could start to expect word-of-mouth sales, or at the very least word-of-mouth approaches. Here was the neighbour of a previous customer calling him up to ask for a quote. They hadn't seen any advertising, but they'd seen his handiwork first hand, and wanted to know more.

Within a week he'd found a customer, built a cubby and sent his first invoice.

The point is that when you start your own business, you need to work out not only what you're going to sell, but how you're going to sell it. It's true that you already have the skills you need to start a business, and it's true that you can develop the skills you need to keep that business ticking over, but as an entrepreneur you need to be prepared to expand your skills.

Partners are a great way to gain quick access to a range of skills you don't already possess, but it's also important to learn from each other and transfer those skills, so that you can carry the business on your own if the need arises.

And there is one essential skill which you must either possess or develop as an entrepreneur: You must be able to find customers. You must be able to share your enthusiasm, sell your product and encourage others to work with you. Even the heads of large successful companies must be ready to switch into sales mode whenever there is a downturn in the market or a new competitor on the horizon.

And while it's easy to look through rose-coloured glasses and assume that everyone who reads your ad will want to buy your product, it's important to keep in mind that they are also seeing the ads of dozens of other suppliers. Running a successful business means figuring out how to attract people to your website, your ad and your service over any other.

Within 12 months, Jenkins had lined up enough work that he was not only able to leave his job, he was also able to hire someone else. Now came the quandary. The obvious choice seemed to be to hire another carpenter so he could focus on building the business. But the whole reason he'd gone into the business in the first place was to work with his hands, doing what he enjoyed.

This is the challenge of momentum for all small business operators. If you do what you do well and build up momentum, you may find yourself no longer doing what you do well, but increasingly tied to the desk carrying out administrative tasks. To grow strategically and to maintain momentum, you need to decide early on how you'll cope with this growth.

Aiming to keep overheads low, he took on a part-time office administrator. Thanks to the internet he was able to create a flexible work-from-home position, and was able to open it up to a young mum returning to work. Rather than employ a qualified carpenter, he took on an apprentice and opted to grow more slowly in the short term in order to take on more work when the apprentice had developed beyond the basic skills.

However, expanding and building on momentum doesn't necessarily mean employing others. When Christina Raul left school halfway through Year 11, her prospects weren't all that good. She knew a little about business and knew she wanted to work with animals, but had long since given up on the hope of getting into a veterinary science degree at university.

So she began with what she knew. Calling in some favours, she managed to turn an old horse float into a mobile dog washing cart. She painted the outside with a paw-print logo and her contact numbers and parked the mobile dog wash van outside her parents' busy shop.

A month later, she'd washed two dogs and hadn't made enough money to pay for the paint, let alone the dog wash trailer. Because she wasn't making any money, advertising in the local paper was beyond her resources. She was on the verge of giving up entirely when she realised her mistake. Although she had a mobile dog wash van, she was expecting her customers to come to her. So, she drove down to the local park and spent a month handing out 'book one, get the second free' vouchers. This approach enabled her to build up a small group of return customers. She also managed to convince the local vet to hand out her flyers to customers, in exchange for washing his own pet dogs.

The next six months saw business boom, which left her with an entirely different problem: she just couldn't physically keep up with the workload. She invested the extra cash flow in another two trailers and began to look for staff, but she just couldn't interest anyone in washing dogs for $12 per hour. When she did find someone, she found she ended up spending far too much time administrating their work and was left with little time to do her own.

She took a week off from work and spent a lot of time thinking about how to find and inspire staff, and asking herself why she enjoyed driving from house to house to wash dogs. How could she inspire others to do the same? Finally she figured it out. She did it, and enjoyed doing it, because it was her business. If she could figure out a way to inspire her staff to consider it *their* business, they might be more interested in actually doing the work. Returning home, she posted an entirely different ad in the paper. Rather than advertising for staff, she offered the opportunity to buy into a dog wash franchise. In theory, this way she made less per van. But in reality, because her franchises turned her staff into owner-operators, they were more motivated and made more sales, so she ultimately made a lot more.

... expanding ... doesn't neccessarily mean employing others.

There are risks with turning your small business into a franchise (there are risks with any sort of growth) and the best way to minimise such risks is to keep in regular contact with staff, partners or franchisees. As you grow, you need to take the time on a weekly basis to fulfil contracts, seek new deals and assess your financial position. This means sitting down and listing your available resources, debtors and creditors to understand your net position. This isn't an added extra. It's important work and needs to be integrated into your weekly timetable.

Knowing to step back and look at your priorities and goals for the business did not come to me straight away. In the early days of my business I found it very difficult to take a step back and really see what was happening around me. I was young and enthusiastic, and always chasing the next deal or opportunity. It wasn't until later, when I had the chance to work with very successful businesspeople, that I really began to understand the importance of taking time out to look at where my business was going. It's not enough merely to keep pushing; you also need to know where you're pushing to.

Creating momentum isn't just about finding more customers ...

It doesn't really matter what business you are in — the only way any business survives is if there's more money coming in than there is going out, and it's not good enough to have a vague idea of these transactions in your head. Taking time each week to look at your financial position might also give you a clearer idea of which of your products and services are doing well and which are doing poorly, which areas need more focus and which are probably better left to subside.

Creating momentum isn't just about finding more customers; it also means regularly assessing where your business is, where it is going, and how you're going to take it there.

Chapter 10

Don't fall into the investment trap

You've got customers, partners, corporate memory, business plans and low-risk approaches to business all covered. I can almost hear that little voice inside your head saying, 'It's all well and good to talk about mitigating risk and looking for partners, but if only I had a big chunk of cash I could get my business idea off the ground'. Most people think like this and wait for years to get the investment they think they need to start the business of their dreams. This is all wrong.

I will tell you a sad story about the true cost of investment. Here's where I say to take that endless curiosity that you need to apply to every aspect of your business and apply it to the businesses you see around you. Before you begin, and at every moment, stop and think about your business from now on.

After almost two decades working as an academic in the university sector, Daryl Douglas received a windfall. He was offered the opportunity to cash in his tenure as a lecturer at the University of Sydney. The golden handshake, while nothing compared to some of the multimillion-dollar deals offered to high-profile CEOs, was enough to pay off his mortgage, give him a nice holiday and tide him over until something else came up.

But that's not what he did. He took the money and invested it in computers, desks, shelving, office space, stationery and all the paraphernalia he'd had access to for free while working at the university. Having already blown most of the money, he set about working with a new communications technology that preceded the internet. Called Videotext, it was a communications system that allowed subscribers to access data via their phone line. Seeing enormous potential, Douglas set about attempting to offer an online news service. Each day he would gather business and political news from a variety of sources and type it out into brief stories and post it onto a Videotext 'website'.

Seeing enormous potential, Douglas set about attempting to offer an online news service.

To a certain degree he was a visionary. He foresaw the information revolution that would take place 10 years later thanks to the internet. He knew office workers would want to glance through the headlines via their computer before reading their correspondence and getting to work. However, he failed to grasp the one idea fundamental to all business: he spent before he made. Armed with a big chunk of start-up capital, he created a structure that was costly and unsustainable. Rather than go to the market to look for buyers, he went to the market to look for sellers and bought up big.

While he fiddled around attempting to figure out what people would pay for the Videotext service, he had to keep spending on rent, electricity, computers, Videotext access, stationery, cards, travel, time and so on.

When news didn't work, he tried racing tips and ran all sorts of other businesses on the side to keep things going. But there just weren't enough people prepared to spend money to get access to the information he was providing online.

Within five years he owed the bank more than twice his initial redundancy payout and was forced into bankruptcy. Both he and his wife lost the superannuation to which they had been contributing since beginning work 25 years before. Anything of resale value disappeared from the house, and a second mortgage was taken out on it. It wasn't pretty.

Okay, enough of the sad stuff. As long as you take away the message that it's downright dangerous to start out a business flush with liquid capital. There's a reason why they describe it as 'cold, hard' cash. Starting out with money means starting out in a totally unrealistic environment. In business it's the needs of others that define your success and, the longer you can afford to pay the rent without focusing on the needs of others, the more likely you are to design systems and goods and services that others simply won't buy.

Liquid capital comes in a poisoned chalice.

Now I can hear all the aspiring café owners letting out an exasperated sigh and tossing this book into the corner because it obviously doesn't deal with businesses that so clearly require a significant initial investment. But the basic principle is universal: find ways to make money without spending it, and you'll do well in business.

Sometimes this means sharing the eventual profits and spreading risks across a number of different people, but meanwhile everyone gets to benefit from the result.

As much as hot-headed speculators will tell you differently, business is not about gambling. It's about minimising and postponing capital investment until you have secured a regular income. It's about investing in a way that's commensurate with your income.

The principle is universal, and can be applied as much to capital-intensive industries as it can to service-based companies. Take Hydrocon Australasia, manufacturers of permeable stormwater pipes, for example. The company was established in the mid 1990s on the basis of German technology that enabled stormwater run-off to be collected and slowly soaked into the ground near where it fell, rather than being piped out to sea.

Having registered the company and obtained an exclusive licence to manufacture the product in Australia, the company's local management needed a way to turn the intellectual capital into a profitable business. They needed to figure out where and how they were actually going to make the pipes. More importantly, they needed to figure out who they were going to sell the pipes to.

Building a brand new plant was out of the question — it would cost millions, and they still didn't know if they had any local customers to sell to. If the pipes were to be made, they would need to find a manufacturing partner with appropriate infrastructure who'd be willing to invest in the new idea.

It was a mixture of shoe leather, curiosity and contacts that saved the day. The curiosity forced them to ask themselves: How can we do this without paying for a new factory? Rather than look for land on an industrial estate, they began talking to contacts all over Australia: real estate agents, business brokers, chambers of commerce, people they'd worked with in the past and people they hoped to work with in the future. Although all this talking

Liquid capital comes in a poisoned chalice.

and networking wore down a significant amount of shoe leather, it cost a fraction of what they would have spent on building an entirely new factory.

Within a couple of months, they were in negotiations with a pipe manufacturer who already had the premises, the corporate knowledge and a customer base of manufacturing outfits. With a pipe factory already operating in a regional city, the manufacturing partners were interested in expanding their line and were able to navigate through all the regulatory hoops that can so easily leave a business floundering.

But even with a manufacturing partner willing and ready, Hydrocon Australasia needed half a million dollars to buy the manufacturing equipment needed to get the product line operational. Rather than taking out a loan and forking out the cash, the fledgling company's directors went in two different directions at once.

On the one hand they started looking for their first customers, figuring the first contract would pay for the infrastructure they needed to get the whole business going. The second thing they needed was the equipment, but rather than pay full price they combed the market for a cheaper machine, thereby minimising their risk.

Eventually they got the machinery they needed from a bankrupt company in Germany for a tenth of the price they would have had to pay if they'd bought it new. At roughly the same time, they managed to sign up their first customers in the Australian market and were able to use the money they'd made from the deal to pay for and import the equipment they needed to fulfil the order.

Partnering, patience and lots of shoe leather provided Hydrocon Australasia with millions of dollars worth of infrastructure at just a fraction of the cost, as well as corporate knowledge and inroads into a customer base. And this kind of no-money-down approach can be applied to just about any type of business, even in capital-intensive industries. All it requires is a little patience and the ability to look for creative opportunities and partnerships.

Rather than looking for a bank manager and indebting yourself, why not look to create mutually beneficial arrangements where other people become involved in making your ideas a success? Look for ways to get others to support your company based on self interest and stay away from spending money. It's not about mitigating risk; it's about removing it from the equation entirely.

A would-be restaurateur might look to partner with a vineyard, a café owner might partner with a neighboring delicatessen to provide prepackaged take-home meals, or a would-be retailer might partner with a shop-fitter to minimise set-up costs. Business is not about gambling; it's about looking for mutually beneficial relationships.

This is a different mindset from traditional business practice; it's one that forces you to adopt realistic, long-term patterns of business. It focuses on solutions rather than problems. And at its base is the idea that no business can operate without customers.

Setting up a business without first setting up a customer base might work, but it's a really risky way to operate and it's the reason why most small businesses go to the wall. Poor choices often result in people losing their livelihoods, their family homes and everything they've worked for. Honest businesspeople who have been through one or two failures will tell you straight: if the business failure cost them money, it affected their family and their health.

Business is not about gambling; it's about looking for mutually beneficial relationships.

But by taking your idea to market before investing in your infrastructure, you effectively let customers decide whether or not your idea is worth investing in—and in the end, it's the customers who will decide your fate. If you take your idea to potential business partners before you take it to market, you have the opportunity to tweak and improve it along the way, minimising the risk of failure.

This allows you to skip over the single issue preventing most people from going into business in the first place:

a lack of liquid capital. Desperate for that initial investment, most people make the mistake of going to the market for very costly cash, which will sooner or later undo them.

Investors and lenders always want their money back, regardless of what it costs the business, and they want it back with a premium. Partners, on the other hand, don't just bring money into a business: they bring knowledge and a vested interest in ensuring the operation is a long-term success. By looking for partners rather than investors you not only fast-track your set-up, you also invite human capital and that all-important corporate knowledge, which would otherwise take a long time to figure out.

Money is not neutral and it's not really what drives business.

By looking for venture capital or business loans you effectively tie a noose around your neck, forcing yourself into regular payments or a fixed timeline without first checking the market to see if it actually wants to turn your idea into a money-making venture.

Money is not neutral and it's not really what drives business. The key drivers are knowing what to do, how to do it and for whom to do it. This is corporate memory, and it's at the heart of all successful companies. It took me more than a decade to realise how powerful corporate memory could be within my business. It's the genetic code of a company, which tells all the separate parts how to operate. Money is the lubricant that keeps you going, but it's corporate memory that gives you the skills you need to keep on going.

In the short term, start-up capital, whether from your own savings, external investors or business loans, gives you a free ride and can set you up for catastrophic failure.

Chapter 11

Time is money, so take your time

So where are we now? We've gone through how important customers are. We've talked about starting out, finding partners, getting infrastructure, getting over your fear of accounting, going to market—oh, and customers, customers, customers.

The problem is that customers, partners and markets don't always respond to our ideas when we want them to. Often they take their time. It's hard to appreciate, when you're excited about your new idea, that not everyone is going to share your enthusiasm—at least not necessarily when you want them to. Often you need to give people time to understand your idea, and how they fit into it, before they are ready to hand over their hard-earned cash.

Remember in chapter 5, where I say the importance of the first meeting is setting up the second meeting? Well, that rule doesn't just apply to customers; it also works for suppliers, partners and even government officials. Don't start selling to people straight away and, for crying out loud, don't expect anyone to share your enthusiasm for a new idea until they've had a chance to think about it. Give it time, and just focus on getting that second meeting.

Tim Fernandez's obsession with the convergence between data and telecommunications is a case in point. Towards the end of the nineties, Tim could see mobile phone and mobile computer technologies converging. He knew there would be fabulous opportunities in the market for a company retailing and distributing mobile telecommunications technology, and for someone who could set businesses up with a complete voice and data mobile communications solution. But no-one would listen. His employer nodded politely but shrugged off his ideas, mobile phone vendors and telecommunications companies seemed disinterested, and computer vendors were much too busy to pay any attention at all.

Sometimes in order for people to understand, you need to show them exactly what you mean. So in 2000 he went into business for himself, and specialised in integrating and servicing mobile communications packages for corporations. Called Technology Connections, the company stayed small while Fernandez continued attempting to convince the rest of the business community of a trend it seemed he and he alone could see developing.

He was still finding it hard to get the large tele-communications companies to take him seriously, so he bought into a Telstra dealership that gave him access to Telstra carrier services. Having armed himself with the connectivity and the gear, he set about creating corporate mobile communications packages just as everybody else started rubbing their eyes and realising there was money to be made.

After three years of pushing his ideas and explaining his plans, everything just fell into place and Technology Connections began to grow at a staggering rate.

Although it had seemed that no-one was listening, all the legwork he'd done suddenly returned to him in the form of business because no-one else in IT integration seemed able to offer the mix of services he'd spent the last couple of years evangelising. Although it seemed like it at the time, his ideas hadn't fallen on deaf ears. What he'd managed to do was sow a seed in not-yet-fertile soil. Once all the other factors fell into place, and the rest of the market woke up to the potential for the technology he'd been talking about, his business was in business in a big way.

… he'd managed to … sow a seed in not-yet-fertile soil.

That example is not quite a path I would necessarily recommend — after all, it involves a lot of risks and setting up shop before getting a single customer — but it's an interesting example of how sometimes ideas just take time before they take off.

Time is money, but sometimes you just need to take your time and wait for everything to fall into place before the market is ready to pay you any money. This is why it's important not to start out in business by borrowing too heavily, or signing anything that will see you paying out before you're actually writing invoices. As long as you don't owe investors or banks too much money, you'll have the time to wait until the market catches up with you.

When Sioned Guard and Sinead Roberts decided to start importing eco-friendly disposable nappies into Australia through their company, ECOdirect, they were confronted with just this challenge. Both had come from high-pressure roles in corporate environments to provide a healthy, eco-friendly alternative to disposable plastic nappies in the Australian market.

The first people they needed to convince were the German-based manufacturers of the nappies. They were reluctant to set up an export relationship with people on the other side of the world who they hardly knew. So Sinead got on a plane and flew to Germany to convince them she meant business. It worked—they won an exclusive import licence—but getting the nappies into Australia was only the first hurdle.

They needed to find their market. They suspected there were parents out there who, like themselves, had kids with particularly sensitive skin, and others who felt guilty about using standard disposable nappies (which take thousands of years to break down in landfill). But with no advertising capital, they needed a creative way to get their message across. So they hit the streets with baskets full of nappies, in search of environmentally conscious mothers. At the same time, the pair took advantage of the vast skills base of friends and contacts that could advise or help them without charging. Getting good advice from experienced people was invaluable — it helped ensure their business had the best chance of succeeding by learning from the mistakes and successes of others. Progress was slow, but eventually the shoe leather paid off as the thousands of nappies they handed out came back in the form of orders.

Environmental concerns, for decades relegated to the economic and political fringe, were increasingly part of the mainstream as seasons of droughts, fires, floods and downright weird weather bore out concerns repeatedly expressed by scientists and activists.

ECOdirect's compostable nappies were the ideal product for parents who were genuinely concerned about their children's health and future, and they responded by placing orders. But it took time for this turnaround to occur. It took time for the parents who'd been posted a trial nappy or had been handed one at a market one day to modify their behaviour, place the call and order through ECOdirect's service. This was all time that Guard and Roberts would not have had if they'd had to pay weekly shopfront rent.

... getting the nappies into Australia was only the first hurdle.

No new idea will be immediately successful — perseverance is the only way to find customers when you are new to a market. So developing a business within its own financial constraints is a basic recipe for survival. The best way to ensure you have the time to find your customers and hold on to your ideas until the market is willing to respond is to set up business structures that require minimum inputs. Don't invest money you don't have on an idea that is unproven.

The market, your customers, are the only decision-makers that matter, and if they don't like your idea or aren't ready to buy into it, no amount of investment will turn it into a profitable enterprise. Do not spend tomorrow's income today. Give yourself the time you need to reach out to the customers and test their response.

Time is money. So save your money, and take your time.

Chapter 12

Take your costs and double them

By now, you have probably figured out that the basic approach to creating a stable, sustainable business is all about keeping your costs to a minimum and focusing on your customers (to the point of becoming ever-so-slightly obsessive).

You know you have a great idea, you know you've got the skills to actually start up a business, but all the great ideas in the world will get you nowhere if you can't balance what you bring into the business with what goes out in terms of expenditure.

While there are lots of underlying reasons why businesses fail, the ultimate cause of the failure is always cash flow. Businesses run out of the money they need to service the bills coming in, usually because they took on those bills without first ensuring that there were lots of customers out there willing to pay them for their goods and services.

When Kristine Bailey set about designing a business plan for her company, Flower Food, she was sure she had everything covered. Having wanted to launch her own business for many years, she finally found the idea she had been looking for. While travelling on an international flight, she had come across an ad for a posy of flowers carved out of fruit. As far as she knew, no-one was offering this kind of gift in the Australian market. She figured that she would have an interesting point of difference over competitors in the corporate and personal gifting space, and that she could survive by using the web as a marketing tool and keeping her overheads low.

With $20 000 in savings, she set out to launch … her idea …

With $20 000 in savings, she set out to launch and rapidly expand her idea into a company. However, with a background in marketing and no hands-on business experience, she knew she'd need to get some help to ensure the business plan was based in reality. Although she didn't realise it at the time, Bailey was taking an enormous risk—the very same risk almost all small businesspeople start out with—taking all her hard-earned funds and sinking them into a product or service that hadn't been tested.

Small companies often make the mistake of wanting to adopt the same approaches and practices as large companies. They want the brand and the infrastructure and the marketing, without first establishing their capacity to actually sell their product. No business, no matter how big or small, survives if it spends more on making and promoting its products than it will make on selling them. Big businesses can occasionally afford to make a loss on individual products because they have usually established that they can make money from selling other products. But small businesses do not have that luxury, and should never shoulder all that extra risk.

Bailey was lucky. In the short term, she had access to a lot of support from friends and family. Having drafted the business plan herself, she went knocking on doors and asked every experienced businessperson she knew to read through it and tell her what they thought.

She aimed to minimise her costs through extensive use of online marketing and by automating as many of her services as possible. Not wanting to lose business to copycats, she wanted to establish herself in lots of cities, as quickly as possible. She knew she would need to spend her modest funds on creating the website and installing commercial kitchens in each city, and opted to invest in technology to do much of the clerical and account-keeping work.

Because orders were placed either online or over the phone, she was able to invoice in advance, and didn't need to fuss around with chasing up payment. By investing in software, she was able to automate most of her back-office business processes and only employ people directly involved in providing services.

However, the one hole in her plan was that she was planning to spend money before she made it. It turned out her costs very nearly prevented her from turning her funky idea into a successful venture. Like the vast majority of aspiring businesspeople, she'd focused on her prices without fully considering her costs. She'd researched her market and she knew how much money people would be willing to spend on this kind of service, but she was terribly mistaken when it came to how much it would cost her to roll her service out.

The one crucial piece of advice she received, as it turned out, came from her mother.

'Would the business still make money if you doubled your costs?' she asked, after reading through the business plan. 'If not, you'd better be careful, because businesses fail when they can't pay their bills.'

Although she had researched the cost of renting and fitting out the facilities she thought she'd need, Baker had forgotten to build in contingency plans or provide much wiggle room for unexpected hold-ups or regulatory requirements that might slow her business down.

Because she'd planned to cover all her costs upfront, she faced a very real danger of losing her life savings due to a single unexpected cost. Luckily for her, she went back to her business plan and redid the numbers from scratch. Taking her mum's advice, she doubled the costings and revised her pricing accordingly—and yes, the business could still make money.

If you can see no other way around paying upfront for facilities, and no other way to find customers than actually developing your business, doubling your costs in your initial business plan is a way to build in wiggle room and focus your attention on the need to make sure every cent you spend on facilities will bring in customers with cold, hard cash. Doubling the costs in your business plan will enable you to adjust your estimates to a worst-case-possible scenario, rather than planning for a perfect run and discovering six months in that retail rents were higher than you initially thought, and being forced to close as a result.

Cash flow (or lack thereof) is what kills most small businesses. The rule of thumb is not to spend money until you're actually making it. This is the most risk-free approach and can be, with a little bit of imagination, applied to most businesses. If you want to open a café, begin with a catering business you can run from home. If you want to start a coaching college, start out tutoring at the local library. If you want to be a personal trainer, don't pay to use a gym; begin to build customers by offering fitness classes in the local park.

... businesses fail when they can't pay their bills.

The most risk-free way to begin your business is to get customers before spending on anything. And this isn't only true of small businesses. Large infrastructure projects such as inner-city office towers, shopping complexes and computer data centres need to have secured an anchor tenant before they go ahead with a build.

Fiona Browne began her corporate training business from her lounge room. She gradually bought the equipment as she won customers, taking her team-building cooking classes to them, rather than taking on the overhead of costly commercial premises.

It wasn't until she had a staff of 15 and a long pipeline of work ahead of her that she was sufficiently confident to rent and fit out premises. And even then a sudden downturn in the economy almost wiped out all her hard work — she was forced to go back to her staff and tell them they might not be employed in the following week.

Rather than putting anyone out of work she cut her own salary back to subsistence wages, reduced hours and put off all extra expenses and projects. Some of her younger staff members left to travel or to take up other opportunities, which took the pressure off, and she became very strategic in the way she spent on advertising. Rather than advertise solidly through the downturn, she held back until the end of the financial year was approaching, then conducted a blitz on all her email contacts, gambling that many organisations would have cut back on expenses through the year and found themselves with a demoralised workforce, and a bit of extra cash.

The gamble paid off. Just as she was seriously considering putting off staff the phone began to ring with last-minute bookings before the end of the financial year.

Many of us go into business with a picture in our minds and mistakenly think that if we fulfil that picture we will be successful. The problem is that the picture isn't the business; that picture is what we want the business to look and feel like. The business only exists insofar as it has customers walking through the door and paying money for your goods and services, regardless of what it looks like.

Your costs can become your downfall unless you know you can keep them under control.

Part II

Negotiation and partnership with the profit principle

Dear Peter,

The year is 1983, and you're now 40 years old. It's been more than 10 years since you first took a step off the precipice and went from being an employee to becoming an entrepreneur.

You've learnt a lot about customers and suppliers, about buying and selling and closing a deal. But the most important lessons are still to come, and these lessons will force you to the realisation that your success is as much about the success and contribution of others.

You are sitting at a table at a gala dinner. You can barely believe you're here among some of the most successful businesspeople, politicians and academics in the country. A huge mining company, BHP, is honouring individuals who have achieved great things in different fields of endeavour. More than 600 nominations have been received, and your name is one of the very few to be among the finalists.

The hum of the cicadas and the casual overalls of that picnic 20 years ago have been replaced by the deafening hum of excited conversation and a formal dinner suit with a bow tie.

You're up against some of the most established and high-profile entrepreneurs in Australian industry. What you don't really understand right now is that you're only here because of other people. You, a migrant who didn't speak English until you were in your twenties, who scrimped and saved for your first van and swept floors and lined up for work in a factory, are sitting among the richest and most powerful people in Australia. Although you don't know it yet, you are about to get the opportunity to become a close friend and associate of people you have only ever seen on TV.

You're about to realise that everything you are and everything you've achieved is the result of your capacity to work with others. What you'll find out in the next 20 years is that success in business is like success in every other aspect of your life—it's not based on who you are and what you can do, but on how you work with those around you.

You are sitting on the forest floor of the most fertile business environment you have ever had the opportunity to witness. You will soon begin to understand that the very tallest trees in the business landscape are those that work in a symbiotic relationship with species that have taken years to grow.

The lights go down. Maggie Tabberer stands at the podium and reads out a list of names, and you just keep on smiling because you never expected to be named among such successful, high-profile people. She smiles and shuffles an envelope and the next few moments are a blinding rush of emotion, lights and noise.

You sit stunned as the spotlight falls on your table, and it is not until your wife prompts you to stand and walk to the stage that you realise that yours was the name that was called out. You don't have time to pinch yourself, as your body takes over and weaves its way in between tables toward the stage. You don't have time to wonder how you got here or what it means, and it's only once you are staring into the blinding stage lights that you recall for an instant the blinding sunlight of a summer's day two decades earlier.

You are speechless, literally. Having been so overwhelmed by being nominated in the first place, you simply didn't bother writing a speech of acceptance, because you know not to trust fairytales.

But here you are, staring into the light, staring at the letters on the trophy—letters proclaiming that the last dozen years of hard work have been noticed, and have been recognised as worthy of note among some phenomenally successful entrepreneurs.

It's only in the wake of this award that you will have the opportunity to really understand that businesses are built for and by people, and that your success will depend on those who work for you, and around you.

It's only in the wake of this award that you will begin to appreciate that you are part of a vast ecosystem of businesses, which depend on each other for their survival.

For the first time since you first stepped out of the comfort of working for others and into the rollercoaster of running your own business, this award will give you the opportunity to work with mentors. People who have been where you are and who are happy to share their mistakes with you.

Slowly you will begin to understand that your way isn't the only way, and that you can learn from mistakes made by others. Initially overwhelmed by their presence you will learn to listen, not just to those who have already achieved success, but to those all around you.

But just for this moment, all I can say to you is this: next time you are nominated for an award, no matter how unlikely you think it is that you will actually win, write a speech and practise saying it until you no longer sound like you've been practising. For my sake.

Sincerest regards,
Peter Fritz
13 May 2010

Chapter 13

We don't need another hero!

Everyone loves a hero: the lone, independent, brave and just individual who single-handedly vanquishes his or her enemies for the greater good. It's an approach that works for Hollywood movies and fairytales, but taking this approach to business is a sure-fire way to make your company fail.

The same goes for those who are going into business to be loved or respected or feared, or anything else. I'd spent over a decade in business before I began to really appreciate the contributions made by those around me, and it wasn't until I stopped working so hard in my business and took a step back to look at other businesses that I realised to what extent others had contributed to my success.

In 1983 I won an award from BHP for excellence in business. At first it gave me a heady, almost punch-drunk sensation as I tried to figure out how it had happened. Gradually it dawned on me that it was only possible because other people had spoken on my behalf. I got to know all kinds of businesspeople, some who had grown up with their family company, and others who were entirely self-made, and working for the first time with business mentors I began to understand some basic facts about business.

The only reason to go into business is to make money. There might be other issues around the periphery, but the main issue is this: without an income there is no business, so making money needs to be a fundamental and ongoing concern. If you're lucky, you'll make that money doing something you love. If you're really lucky, it will also lead to some greater good — but don't let visions of grandeur get in the way of your profit and loss summaries. And while you might not yet be wearing your underpants outside your pants, or flitting around the office in a cape, chances are you're limiting your own progress by adopting heroic attitudes when a more cooperative approach is required.

The only reason to go into business is to make money.

The most successful businesspeople are not the ones who achieve everything themselves; they are usually the ones who are the best at gathering human resources and capital and getting it all marching towards a common goal. The secret to achieving all this lies not in heroics but in your willingness to drop the bravado and work with others.

You already know about the importance of finding customers and the power of using partnerships to gain knowledge, skills and services. Well, the connecting point that ties all of these elements together is a willingness to seek out the skills and opportunities around you. It's a willingness to work with others, and not attempt to take all the glory for yourself.

Bravado leads to arrogance, and arrogance prevents you from working effectively with others. It prevents you from considering and listening to the ideas of partners, suppliers, employees or customers. And the belief that you can do everything alone will prevent you from seeing the easier, cheaper and quicker ways to get the job done.

Heroes don't work well with others; they just try to do everything themselves. Usually they succeed, because they have magical powers. But you don't have magical powers, and you live in the real world and not in a comic book. So throw away your cape, and take a look at the skills the people around you have.

The first thing to remember is that all aspects of business involve working with others. Customers, partners, suppliers, employees—every transaction and every exchange involves a certain degree of compromise. But if you start out with the assumption that this compromise will inexorably lead to you giving ground or conceding in some way, then you are likely to miss out on some important opportunities.

Always enter into business conversations assuming you will be able to extract more from the arrangement than you would be able to achieve alone. By working together and looking for complementary arrangements, you can actually increase the size of the pie you are looking to divide—so everyone wins. Enlarging the pie requires a whole different mindset to wanting to win at all costs, and the unfortunate reality of business is if your focus is on winning at all costs, you'll probably end up losing in the long run.

Take the example of the shipment of oranges that comes into port, having been mistakenly sold to two separate customers. Both face losing their business if the shipment is not processed within days of reaching port so, without discussing the issue further, they agree to split the shipment in two and await a second shipment to fill the rest of their order.

But if they had bothered to investigate further, they would have discovered their activities were entirely complementary. One company produced juice and was only interested in the pulp, and the other threw away the pulp and juice in order to produce candied peel. Had they discussed the arrangement, they might not only have been able to keep the entire shipment but gone on to make substantial savings on future shipments.

... start to look at the problem from both sides.

Working with others isn't always this neat, and complementarities are rarely this obvious, but invariably you can come up with more through working closely with others, always with the view to actually finding solutions, than you would by simply setting out to win at all costs.

This is especially true when looking for the sorts of partnerships we've already discussed. With a little creativity you can get a lot more out of a partnership than you start with in the first place. If you begin by assuming the negotiation process will in fact enhance your opportunities, you will also start to look at the problem from both sides. Always attempt to offer proposals that are in the best interests of the other party. Go to them and speak to their priorities, rather than focusing on your own. Don't start out with a proposal, start with the intention of listening to and understanding the requirements of the other party, whether they are a supplier, a business partner or customer, or even a government agency.

Perhaps you won't come away from the first meeting with a proposal—maybe it will just be a sounding-out process—but as long as you organise to meet again, you'll both have the opportunity to think about how your businesses could work together.

Take the gym at the base of an office block. The gym owner is looking to recruit members from what he sees as a captive market, so he goes to one of the companies in the office block and offers individual patrons a good deal on memberships. He gets a small increase in membership, but it soon withers away.

Having thought about it, he tries again. This time he books in to see one of the business owners who rents space in the office block and has a casual chat about the demands on his business. As it turns out, the owner of the business would like his staff to stay fit and active, because he believes it will make them more productive, but he has discouraged them from joining the gym, worried that it would eat into their work time. Back in his office, the gym owner designs a membership plan whereby company employees are provided discounted membership if they use the gym at specified times of the day. The business owner is so pleased with the arrangement that he agrees to further subsidise the membership costs, and include gym membership as part of the annual bonus given to especially productive employees. Staff morale gets a boost and absences due to illness are reduced, improving productivity, while the gym boosts its membership.

Minimise risk, share the rewards. None of this is about power, trickery or domination — none of this is about magic, capes or heroics. It's all about looking for people who'll work together with you toward a common goal. The most successful businesses are those that find creative ways to partner with other businesses and recruit the most effective people in each field and inspire them toward a shared outcome.

To succeed in business, the whole must be greater than the sum of its parts.

Chapter 14

Talk is cheap, so keep on talking

By now you're probably wondering when I'm going to get to some of the more practical aspects of running a business. I could always stop here and explain how to fill out a profit and loss sheet, but what's more interesting, and often missing from existing books on business, is why one business gets a sale when another misses out, or why one entrepreneur finds the right partners while another struggles through inappropriate and often damaging business deals.

While lawyers will tell you it all comes down to the way contracts are drafted, and accountants will tell you it's all about how payment mechanisms are designed, the truth of the matter is that businesspeople do business with other businesspeople, and closing a deal is mostly about winning the trust of those around you.

Opportunities to meet new people who may determine the direction of your business occur all the time, and are often random and unplanned. Creating business opportunities may be as simple as exchanging pleasantries in a lift, or sending out personalised Christmas cards. The most successful entrepreneurs and businesspeople have an innate understanding of the importance of every single human associated with their brand and their company.

Whether or not they are conscious of it, they are well aware that no-one succeeds in business without the ability to access a vast array of different skills and connections, and the broader your connections, the more chance you'll have of being successful.

In the same way great salespeople understand it's more important to keep the customer than it is to close the sale, great entrepreneurs understand that it's more important to keep up the dialogue than it is to close the deal. They will also network tirelessly and strategically, integrating the process of meeting people into the way they conduct business. Strategic networking means going out there and getting to know not just a small handful of people who are potential suppliers, customers or partners, but getting out there and getting to know people on the off chance they may *become* potential suppliers, customers or partners.

Times were tough for Sue Jaques. The up-market café she'd opened in a sleepy beach suburb was not getting the regular clientele she'd expected. She needed to create alternative streams of income, and thought a catering business would be the best option to do so—but she lacked the marketing budget to launch one.

Just as she was contemplating closing her doors, something extraordinary happened. One of the delivery drivers who regularly dropped off meat and produce stopped by and passed on the details of a family friend who needed a new caterer for his events business and reception hall in a neighbouring suburb. The driver had never been a paying customer, but would occasionally share a steak sandwich with the chef after dropping off an order, and although Jaques never expected it to lead to any work, she simply believed in the importance of treating everyone who came into contact with the café with respect. Thanks to her courteous way of conducting her business, she (unknowingly) had forged the connection that ultimately saved her café.

... closing a deal is mostly about winning the trust of those around you.

The realisation that all businesses operate within an extensive ecosystem of other interdependent businesses has some profound implications for the way you conduct yourself in every interaction and at every phase of your operations. Every conversation you have, whether formal or informal, reflects back on your business. The way you treat someone today will have ramifications for the way they treat your business tomorrow.

What saved Jaques's business wasn't a classy marketing campaign, it was her own innate sense that everyone who interacted with her business needed to come away with a positive impression, regardless of whether they were customers, cleaners or delivery drivers. And certainly the most successful businesspeople do this without thinking; they are unfalteringly polite, patient and generous with their time, realising that the courier who turns up with a package today may well be a potential business partner tomorrow.

In fact, this very book is the result of people knowing people. The fundamental principles come from me, Peter Fritz, but these ideas are illustrated and recorded using the writing of Jeanne-Vida Douglas. It's a weird combination really, a 30-something working mum and a 70-something entrepreneur, and the only reason we came together is that we both keep our eyes and ears open to others.

I wanted to write a book to help others understand how businesses establish themselves and grow, and Jeanne-Vida wanted to write a book to gather all of the stories she heard and recorded in more than 10 years working as a business journalist, talking to some of the most and least successful businesspeople in the country. We had both run our own businesses, and were intensely familiar with the experiences of others.

In fact, this very book is the result of people knowing people.

The only thing we had to go on when we first met was the mutual desire to communicate what we'd learnt, and a mutual friend in Tamara Plakalo. As we both trusted Tamara, her taste, her intelligence and her recommendations, we began meeting to discuss ideas. And the more we talked the more we realised that my experiences over decades in business reflected exactly the day-to-day anecdotes of triumph and tragedy that Jeanne-Vida covered in her work.

There was no reason for us to come together except that we had a mutual interest in communicating our ideas and experiences, and no way would we have come together if it weren't for our contact with others. This symbiosis of mutual interest and complementary skills underpins just about every successful partnership.

Ultimately what the most successful businesspeople realise is that by getting out there and meeting people, and leaving a favourable impression behind them, they are minimising the risks associated with running a business. The most stable businesses are those that can count on the goodwill they have generated over years of positive interaction with customers and suppliers. In business terms, it's the market value of a company minus its tangible assets; it's the extra amount customers and investors are willing to pay for a share of the company based on its reputation in the market and the community.

A happy customer (or partner or supplier) will come back and create positive feedback about your company, while a dissatisfied customer (or partner or supplier) is not only unlikely to return to your business, they may very well prevent others from turning up in the first place.

Oddly enough, it's during the toughest of economic times that this goodwill really makes a difference to the way people relate to your company. If you can plan for networking and relationship development to be part of your business strategy from the very beginning, you are more likely to build a stable business with a strong, loyal customer base in the long term.

In tough economic times, companies and individuals cut back on consumption. But interestingly, they take an emotional approach to cutting back, rather than a purely economic one. In tough times, consumers turn not to the cheapest brands on the market, but rather to brands they trust. They seek comfort over savings, and it's during these downturns that the brands with the most accumulated goodwill outperform their rivals.

A broad network of customers, contacts and alliances is so fundamental to the long-term success of your company that you actually need a targeted relationship development plan. Associates who hold your business in high esteem are able to provide all manner of investment, advice, customers and commercial information. More importantly, these sorts of associates are able to put you in contact with others who might be able to expand your business further still. One positive verbal reference from someone who is already familiar with your services is worth any number of cold calls, and for this reason your contacts list needs to be regularly updated and maintained.

But if all this seems overwhelming, there are some simple rules which are both easy to follow and highly effective in creating large networks of potential customers, partners and associates.

The first is to treat each and every meeting as an opportunity to add to your network. Always make an effort to be sociable and reliable, and treat everyone you come across with the respect and courtesy you would expect from others. Always treat those you meet as potential contacts and, even if you never meet again, take the opportunity to ask their views and opinions on business. And listen closely, even if the idea is not relevant to your own business. Finally, don't treat networking like a necessary evil. Enjoy speaking with people, be open and genuine in your interest. Good networks require sincerity, integrity and a genuine exchange of information, otherwise they will appear false and ultimately have a negative impact on your reputation. After all, none of us would be here, reading or writing this book, if it weren't for the power of good experiences and a willingness to talk and listen to others.

The hand that you shook last week, last month or last year might well be the one that leads to your next deal. So go out and shake a few more hands.

Chapter 15

Don't talk until you see the whites of their eyes

Having combated the myth that businesses are driven by hardy, independent heroes, we need to look at what skills an entrepreneur actually needs in order to advance their business. And while every single interaction will reflect in some way on your business, there are some that will be crucial to its success, and these need to be handled with particular care.

The next thing you need is the ability to work with others, and this almost always involves negotiation. In fact negotiation is one of those non-negotiable skills that all successful businesspeople need to master.

Negotiation skills are a little like sales skills; they are both fundamental to the role of the entrepreneur. Negotiation skills are useful at every level of business, whether it's working with suppliers, finding partners, employing new staff or securing a new contract. Although you'll need to get out there and get some practice, there are some starting points that will make the process of acquiring those skills a little less traumatic.

At just 18, with no start-up capital and a pile of flyers printed up on a school computer, Gareth Vaughan started his own company. His saleable commodity was a skill he had discovered almost by accident; he was able to make people relax so deeply they went into a trance-like state.

While in this deeper state of relaxation, they appeared to be amenable to all sorts of suggestions, which they would incorporate into their behaviour upon waking. Essentially what he had stumbled on was the capacity to hypnotise people. Intrigued by his knack, he decided to complete a diploma in clinical hypnotherapy during his final year at high school and, through word of mouth, found some customers who wanted to quit smoking or lose weight. However, he was keen to apply the technique to the corporate environment and needed a way in.

... always negotiate decision-maker to decision-maker.

Working one on one, or with small groups, Vaughan created guided meditation sessions designed to help executives, managers and call centre staff relax and approach decision-making with a clearer, more focused mind. Still facing very limited resources, Vaughan extended his marketing to include industry summits and expos, and found himself presenting at a human resources summit in Sydney in March 2006. He pulled out all he could muster to pitch his service, market his abilities and sell his skills. The response was pretty encouraging; after speaking with a range of people in the crowd, he felt sure he'd come away from the event with some new corporate customers.

But when the time came to actually sign up for the service, the contacts he'd built up seemed to disappear. He'd leave messages and attempt to get back in contact with them, but the enthusiastic responses had apparently evaporated. The simple fact was the people he'd spent so much time and energy convincing weren't the people who would ultimately sign the cheques. They were enthusiastic and keen to try the service, but when it came to selling the idea to their bosses, they were unable to capture the idea in quite the way Gareth had presented it in the first place. Their pitches had been overridden.

Vaughan learnt an important lesson, and he learnt it the hard way; never waste your time pitching to someone who can't actually pay you for it.

The first principle of negotiation is simply this: always negotiate decision-maker to decision-maker. The moment you negotiate with someone who has no authority to commit, you place yourself in a weaker position. You offer up your priceless business ideas to someone who does not really know how to integrate them into their own company's operations. Underlings, intermediaries and personal assistants might be very well meaning, but they won't be able to make a decision and they are unlikely to do your ideas justice when they repeat them later on. This is not to say that you shouldn't treat everyone with respect and attentiveness—as I say in chapter 14, that's integral to your success—but leave the negotiation itself to the people who have the power to actually make the decisions.

Good negotiation skills are fundamental to minimising your risk and maximising your potential for success in business. It's through negotiation skills that you will make the connections you'll need to survive. So here are some quick crib notes on negotiation to get your creative juices flowing.

The first principle of negotiation we've covered: only negotiate decision-maker to decision-maker. But there's another component to this principle: don't say a word until you see the whites of their eyes. Emails, phone calls and, heaven forbid, text messages are simply too easy to dismiss. Save your energy and ideas for when you can actually meet face to face with someone who can make a decision.

The second principle of negotiation is that there are *always* choices available, and it's up to you as a negotiator to find out what these choices are. If you go into a nego-tiation assuming you already know the outcome, you are probably doomed to begin with. Whereas if you go into a negotiation assuming that you will, by working together, reach a new and better conclusion than any you can think up right now, you'll be surprised by what you'll be able to achieve.

Negotiation is a process through which you arrive at a conclusion that benefits both parties. Negotiation is a process of discovery and revelation where you seek to discover ways to increase the size of the cake you will ultimately divide.

By going into a negotiation with a clear and concrete idea of what you want to get out of it, you can potentially limit the success of the endeavor. As with business meetings, don't set out with a concrete goal or timetable; set out on a journey of discovery, seek information from fellow negotiators, and look for ways you can work together. Negotiation is the path you'll take to realise the full potential of your business ideas, so be prepared to change and grow through the process.

by working together ... you'll be surprised by what you'll be able to achieve.

The third principle of negotiation is: focus on the fundamental challenge, not the personalities involved.

In any negotiation, there will be different motives for each participant, but analysing individuals rather than focusing on the problem at hand is a great way to get sidetracked. Always focus on what it is that brings you together in the first place; analyse the problem, and look for creative, joint solutions.

You want to refit a shopfront in order to open a restaurant for the lowest cost possible; the shopfitter wants a month's work for a standard payment. On the surface, they appear to be two entirely different and irreconcilable needs, which could only be bridged by a financial transaction that benefits one negotiator at the expense of the other.

However, by simply stating the problem in conventional terms you will often make the space between the supplier and buyer a vast gulf when it could in actual fact be a small leap. Perhaps the shopfitter's partner or son is a keen cook and would be interested in coming into the business as well. Perhaps the shopfitter would be interested in using the installation as a test bed for design ideas she believes will work in your favour. Perhaps the shopfitter will be able to line up second-hand or recycled materials that would serve not only to cut costs, but to also create an interesting atmosphere in the restaurant.

Begin by stating the problem: we need a shop fit-out. Then start to look for creative solutions, rather than simply asking for a quote. By bringing suppliers closer into your business, you will be able to draw on their industry knowledge and gain insight into aspects of operations you never considered.

Think about it this way: a shopfitter with a decade or more of experience will have developed a very good sense of which retail outlets are likely to work, and which will struggle to attract customers. Once you get yourself into the business through a negotiation mindset, the possibilities will start to seem endless. We all want different things, and it is because of these different goals, rather than in spite of these different goals, that we are likely to work well together.

... start to look for creative solutions, rather than simply asking for a quote.

Which brings us to the fourth principle of negotiation: play chess, not poker. If you're serious about working with someone, then they need to know where you stand; you need to show them your pieces.

Playing poker is a great way to end up doing business with a bunch of secretive scam artists, because that's effectively the way you're behaving. Chess, on the other hand, necessarily means showing people where you are at the moment, but not necessarily where you're going.

Negotiation is a game based on integrity and strategy, not on secrecy and subterfuge. If you want to bring talented people in to work alongside you, you first need to demonstrate that you can be trusted. As soon as the other person senses you have a card up your sleeve, you lose their trust, and very probably their business. Negotiation is still a self-interested process; you play chess to win, but the most skilful negotiators are those who can reach an outcome about which both parties feel good.

Oddly enough, in negotiation you probably assume that your greatest challenge is sitting across the table, when in fact it is inside your own skin. People often begin the negotiation with themselves and beat themselves before they're even started, rather than putting forth the challenge and beginning the negotiation with the other person.

On a sunny Sydney afternoon, Hydrocon Australasia found itself with a bit of a dilemma. A truckload of enormous pipes had arrived at its modestly sized inner-city offices. Thanks to a last-minute cancellation, there was no customer to deliver to and nowhere to store the pipes until a new customer was found.

The company had signed another distribution agreement, although the newly appointed partner was not expecting a delivery until later in the month. Hydrocon's chief purpose was to find a quick and inexpensive way to store the pipes until they could be sold, so simply by taking an early delivery of the pipes the distributors would have been doing the company a substantial favour.

So, here's the fifth principle of negotiation: don't start the negotiations before the negotiations start.

Given Hydrocon was looking to move the pipes, and the sooner the better, it would have been too easy to set out with the assumption that the distribution company was in fact doing them a favour. However, by beginning the negotiations before the negotiations actually began Hydrocon may well have lost the opportunity to invoice the distributor from the time the pipes were actually collected. Hydrocon's problem was where to store the pipes; the distributor's problem was where to get stock. The situation may have been entirely complementary for both parties.

By having a conversation with ourselves before we have a conversation with the other party, we'll often limit ourselves to fulfilling our personal vision of the situation, and lose out on important information and opportunities. Don't make the mistake of thinking that a negotiation is all about fulfilling your own requirements, because you'll generally limit the opportunity to achieve much, much more.

Any deal that seems too good to be true probably is...

Finally then we get to the sixth and last principle of negotiation: don't fall for the set-up!

One of the things we'll look at in the next chapter is the fact that the only person who is considering your wellbeing in business is you. So when someone comes to you with information that seems to demand an immediate response, take a deep breath and make sure you have all the facts before doing anything.

Bad decisions are generally made too quickly and on the basis of insufficient information, and bad decisions are what someone is hoping you'll make if you are unfortunate enough to find yourself in a set-up. As I said earlier: time is money, so take your time, find out all the information and avoid a set-up. Any deal that seems too good to be true probably is too good to be true.

No business survives, and none thrive, without good solid negotiation skills on the part of the entrepreneur. But like the sports star, the entrepreneur needs to practise them regularly in order to hone their skills and succeed in business.

Now that you have read through the theory, it's your chance to go out and apply it in the real world. And don't be disappointed if you don't achieve what you think you should when you first set out. Return to the principles and focus always on the new outcome which can only be achieved by those who are able to look beyond their initial desires to a new, mutually beneficial conclusion. Your challenge is to find that conclusion.

Chapter 16

Pick your battles, and prepare for peace

You may have heard the term 'soft skills' used to refer to personal interactions—the capacity a person has to reach agreement with others, or to convince other people to behave in this way, or accept that idea.

This is a very stupid term. There's nothing 'soft' about these skills—they are in fact very hard. They are hard to learn, hard to implement, hard to measure and hard to maintain. But to be successful, you must develop these 'hard' skills. You must cultivate the ability to speak with people and express your ideas, and to encourage people to think and act in certain ways, whether it's to buy your products, work for you, provide you with a service, or sell you their company.

Several years ago I found myself on a plane landing at Charles de Gaulle Airport on the outskirts of Paris. My task was seemingly impossible, but worth a good deal of money—enough at least to warrant me flying to the other side of the world.

One of the companies my colleagues and I founded made software for very large utilities. The software was very complex and costly, and on this

My task was seemingly impossible, but worth a good deal of money ...

occasion not only had the customer not paid us, they somehow managed not paid us, they somehow managed to lose any trace of their obligation to do so. It was a large and bureaucratic company and the people we had sold the software to in the first place had long since moved into new roles. I had lots of documentation, no contacts within the company and an invoice for $800 000, which I somehow needed to deliver.

Negotiations always have a period of going badly. Even negotiations that apparently arrive at a satisfactory conclusion have to pass through a time of difficulty, of challenges, claims and counterclaims. The trick is to find a way to work through these challenges to a point where you can actually progress.

In this case the lowest point was the very beginning. I set off to meet the new general manager knowing full well that, for him, success in this scenario would be to reach a point where I went away empty-handed.

Two days later I again boarded a plane. Not only had the $800 000 been released, but the company once again become a customer. How was this possible? Because

I realised I needed to present the new general manager with a proposition that would enable both of us to win the conflict. He would be able to pay as long as he secured something of value for his company, and I gained twice: winning the payment and renewing a lapsed customer.

Business is about making money, but you don't do business with money—you do it with people. Every personal interaction you carry out needs to be tackled with a certain level of respect and courtesy. There are some interactions that need thorough preparation and planning if you're going to achieve the best outcome for your business. The most damaging and destructive business battles are commonly the result of failed negotiations. Good negotiation skills are rarely taught in schools or universities, and like many aspects of business they are largely picked up through observation and experience.

But there is a useful, if rather long, checklist of approaches that can be applied to just about any situation. Negotiations aren't always fraught affairs—they can be short and effective, but they can also drag on for weeks and months without resolution, which is often worse than not having opted to negotiate in the first place.

The most important thing to remember is that business negotiations are carried out between people, and unless these people are well matched and well informed, it will be nearly impossible for them to reach a consensus. Before going into a negotiation, make sure you know who you'll be talking to—and do your homework. Find out as much as you can about their business track record, as well as their reputation. Find out if they have any interests or hobbies, as this knowledge may give you the opportunity to deflect conflict if it arises at any point during the negotiation. Where possible, try to match the personality of the negotiators. Although small-business owners have few options available to them, a particularly difficult or important negotiation might be the perfect occasion to call in some favours from the extensive network of contacts you've established.

These sorts of measures will help to ensure that personal conflicts don't get in the way of reaching a positive outcome. But personality alone won't be enough to affect the outcome. It's also important to set the context for the negotiation prior to any meeting actually taking place. Make sure that every party has a clear understanding of the purpose of the negotiation, and that all parties are participating in the exchange because they believe they will be able to reach a favourable outcome. Be clear about your purpose, and be clear about what matters are to be discussed and resolved, and which can be left alone. Prior to going into the negotiation, it is also crucial to identify the key points of disagreement, and have a clear idea of which areas might be more flexible than others.

After a very challenging week, Andrew Holmes received a phone call from his telecommunications provider. He was informed that he would need to pay extra for services he was already receiving due to some technical glitch that had seen him undercharged. Furious, Holmes launched into a tirade, refusing to pay the money and threatening to switch to a new supplier. He hung up on the caller. For a couple of days he continued to avoid their calls, and it wasn't until a new bill arrived that he realised the increased charge was minuscule, and that the initial caller had in fact wanted to switch him over to a more effective contract. Had Andrew opted to negotiate rather than retaliate, he would have discovered the solution was not only achievable, it was beneficial to both parties.

Negotiations should always focus on the practical aspects of the deal. Andrew initially refused to negotiate, not wanting to accept what he felt was an unjust charge, and as a result he initially missed the opportunity to simply pay the charge and receive a new service. Rather than adopting set principles, always bring into a negotiation a very clear picture of what you would like to achieve, and what you believe the other parties will also be able to achieve. But remember, unless you are willing to shift these expectations, you are unlikely to achieve anything useful. A negotiation isn't about getting what you want, or 'winning a deal' in the traditional sense, it's about finding a new solution that caters sufficiently to all parties.

Negotiations should always focus on the practical aspects of the deal.

It's important to set time frames for the conclusion of talks to create a sense of urgency, and quite simply because it will be impossible to reach any conclusion unless you set out initially to define it. It's often worthwhile seeking a commitment principle from all parties prior to engaging in any direct negotiation. This is a simple statement that outlines the area that is to be discussed, the deadline and some basic conditions surrounding the potential agreement, the expectation that a positive agreement can be reached for all parties, and a commitment to maintaining a good working relationship between all parties. Most negotiations that fall apart do so not because there is no way of reaching a conclusion acceptable to both parties but because of an issue regarding the method of the negotiation, or confusion regarding the role and responsibilities of the individual negotiators.

What all this boils down to is: do your homework, and understand what the expectations are and what the outcomes will be. There is always a resolution to any conflict, and your job in a negotiation is to discover what that resolution might be. If there are some areas where you are not able to be flexible, offer to compensate by being more flexible in others, and go into the meeting knowing that you're able to reach an outcome that is acceptable to both parties. In fact, it may well be something neither of you had considered previously.

There is always a resolution to any conflict...

Lastly, remember that good negotiation is the cheapest, fastest and most effective way to solve any business problem. It gives you the chance to turn an antagonist into an ally, and is vastly underestimated in a world of business that is unfortunately dominated by legal disputes.

The only way to ensure that a negotiation has a successful outcome for all participants is to go into the meeting with a clear brief and an expectation to surpass the expectations of others.

Chapter 17

What's in it for me?

Business isn't about stuff. It's about people. In fact, people are fundamental to the success of any business, even though they often get lost in the numbers and the jargon of modern management techniques.

Sometimes business is about getting stuff from one lot of people and shipping it to another and sometimes it's about providing services people want, but regardless of the specifics, it's always about working closely with people towards some kind of shared goal.

And identifying shared goals is not always easy. Whether it's a partner, a customer, an investor, an employee or a supplier you're talking to, it's always important to start out by establishing a shared basis from which you are both working, and identifying where you are both heading.

Forcing people to do things isn't good business, and in many cases it's illegal, so it's a bad idea. The sweet spot you need to find is the one where you and the person on the other side of the table have different but complementary motivations for committing to a transaction. This kind of relationship is obvious in a retail setting. You want to sell your stock for money within a set period of time, and your customer wants some milk for breakfast. The price is agreed upon when the customer takes the milk out of the fridge and glances at the tag. The customer pays you money, they take their milk — there's no coercion and everyone is ultimately happy with the transaction.

Or are they?

It's not enough in business to sell one litre of milk to one person. Businesses only work when they sell several litres of milk to several people; when people are happy not just to come once, but to come back repeatedly. They're not just paying for the milk, either — they are paying for the convenience, the smile, the clean shop, all the extras that make it worth not just coming once, but coming time and time again.

The smile is a fundamental part of the transaction, because you're not selling milk to a faceless automaton — you're selling milk to another person, and they'll decide where to carry out their next transaction on the basis of this current transaction. The key to doing business is to remember that you're doing it with people, and if you want them to keep coming back you need to make it in their interests to do so. You need to make their experience pleasant and easy.

This goes double for finding and securing partners and suppliers. Take, for example, a company called Costec. It didn't start out as a company, it started as a piece of software designed to be used on mini-computers (this was back when they were still state-of-the-art technology).

The challenge was simple. With a starting capital of zero, the two business partners would attempt to steal market share from a clutch of billion-dollar companies. And in actual fact, they didn't even start out with the software. They had little else but a notion of what they might like to build and, of course, the skills to build it. So they strapped on their shoes and started knocking on doors. But oddly enough, no-one was interested in buying into a non-existent technology.

Forcing people to do things isn't good business...

So, they went and changed their pitch. Rather than going to potential end users, they went to the federal government, based on the assumption that the government grant board for science and research might furnish them with the capital they needed to get the project off the ground.

Six months later, their first customer was the federal government. While it wasn't in the least bit interested in buying their software, it had granted them $600 000 to create an Australian company to give smart people work opportunities, and hopefully use the technology as the basis to create a big company that would pay back the grant in taxes. This grant, however, was provided on the basis that Costec would contribute a further $600 000 in cash or kind, and the kind they put in came in the form of software development.

A matter of months later, Costec had been formed as a company and was armed with a software prototype that would allow energy generators, such as power stations, to run complex simulations and plan for future developments based on the results. The idea wasn't original; there were already products on the market that did just that. But it was different insofar as it ran on less-expensive technology and was, in itself, vastly less expensive than the other products already available.

It's not market failure, it's just human nature.

With the government funding just about to run out, they pitched their product to a power station in Western Australia going to tender for exactly this kind of simulation technology. Here's where the rational decision-making process can look entirely irrational from the outside. Despite offering the least expensive and most technologically advanced solution, Costec lost the bid to a vastly more expensive offer from Toshiba.

Why? Well, the rational reality of the market is that purchasing decisions are rarely based just on price or technological prowess. When it comes to spending millions of dollars of company money, most managers will opt to go with products that they know and products that make them feel safe. It's not market failure, it's just human nature.

Costec faced the challenge of attempting to enter a market dominated by large and well-established companies. It's almost impossible for a small company to compete against a large company, even if their products are cheaper and of a better quality, simply because they lack the credibility they need to win the sales.

But fear not; our story doesn't end here. Because Costec was operating on such low costs, they were able to invest all their skills and resources into selling the software. Thanks to the government grant there was enough money coming into the company already to cover their most basic costs, but they needed to expand their customer base without expanding their cost base if they were going to survive into the next quarter.

The Costec developers continued to network among potential buyers until finally they came into contact with a French company, Thompson CSF, with a particularly interesting challenge. In order to continue to provide power station infrastructure to the Australian government, Thompson CSF needed to find an Australian partner. They needed to show the federal government that a certain percentage of their business was going back into the local economy. Based in France, Thompson CSF had contracts with power stations all over the world and, sure enough, Costec was able to piggy-back on this global presence and massively expand its footprint into other markets. So this second customer wasn't merely a customer — it was also a means to an end for Costec, which now had the means to access power stations all over the world.

This brings us to a very important point: if you are a small company and you want to be a large company, you can flog yourself, developing access to markets over a number of years, only to be bought out by a larger company anyway. Or, and this is the much more interesting option, you can look for a big partner who already has the connections you need to get your product out there.

Developing access to markets is very costly and time consuming, and you can end up perpetually chasing a market without ever actually catching it. Partnerships are a great shortcut to establishing the reputation and credibility you need.

If our first rule is to find a customer, then our second is to get yourself alongside other companies that have access to customers, and mooch off some of their credibility and market access. Customers sometimes react in ways that seem entirely irrational to the outside world, because they are responding to some kind of internal logic. Often the best response is to get inside their heads by partnering with a company that already has them figured out.

As for Costec, it ended up with customers in China, Thailand, Singapore, Malaysia, Korea, India, Egypt, Zimbabwe, South Africa, the UK, Germany, France, the US and Mexico. It was listed on the ASX, and was last seen morphing into a separate company called UXC, with reported revenues of $300 million in 2006.

So, as long as both parties have an interest in working together, the relationship can be long term and profitable. But more on this later.

By looking at a transaction as simply an exchange of goods for money, you're missing both the point and probably the most lucrative elements of the exchange process. Each interaction provides you with the opportunity to stimulate more frequent and more profitable interactions in the future. And this means forgetting your needs for a moment and focusing firmly on the needs of the other party. By focusing on the other person's interests, rather than your own, you have more chance of presenting them with a proposal they will find attractive.

It's seldom easy, and never wise, to convince someone who does not want to be convinced. So the first step is to whet their appetite in some way, test the water and make sure what you're about to offer will actually be worthwhile.

Margaret Grayson, a keen gardener and grandmother, found herself staying with her daughters and grandkids in a holiday house in a beachside town for a family wedding. The house and views were wonderful, but the garden was a mess: a bare lawn encircled by patches of struggling shrubs, overgrown with weeds. So, she spent some of her holiday time pulling up weeds and pruning the neglected trees.

Partnerships are a great shortcut to establishing the reputation and credibility you need.

A month or so later she was contacted by the house's owners who thanked her for the work she'd done. Thinking fast, she offered to return with her family during the quieter periods of the year and maintain the garden in exchange for a discounted rental.

The solution was perfect. Margaret got a regular holiday to spend time with her grandkids and do some gardening, while the owners got their garden maintained and were able to rent out the house when it would otherwise have been left empty. The solution worked because there was something in it for everyone. And it's a perfect example of the sort of solutions you need to look for in business. If you want people to work with you, you need to make it in their interests to do so, and their interest isn't always financial.

A classic example is the provision of training through an apprenticeship. The tradesperson agrees to dedicate a significant amount of time transferring their skills to an apprentice; the apprentice forgoes potential earnings in exchange for the skills they are picking up along the way. As the apprentice learns and becomes more reliable, the tradesperson can share their workload

Business isn't just about buying low and selling high…

and pitch for more business while the apprentice gradually earns more and ultimately becomes fully qualified. The agreement works because both parties have a vested interest in fulfilling the arrangement.

Business isn't just about buying low and selling high; it's about identifying mutually beneficial arrangements and using them to improve your bottom line. This is especially relevant to the risk reduction or partnering technique I discuss in chapter 7. By sharing the business, you share the risks and rewards. But in order to share the business, you often have to start by explaining what the risks and rewards are likely to be, not just for you, but also for your potential partners.

Once you have identified the skills you need to add to your business, finding those skills often comes down to figuring out what the business can offer your potential partners, rather than focusing on what they can do for you.

Making people want to do business with you isn't about you or the products you offer, it's about them, and what they want to achieve. A common mistake is to go into a sales meeting talking about yourself and what you want, rather than doing your research and finding out what they want and using the meeting to make the connection.

If you've been focusing firmly on what you can get from others, why not try a different approach and start thinking about what they might want you to do for them? In most cases, it will force you to look at the problem from an entirely different angle, and perhaps begin to see yourself the way others see you. What are you to their business? Are you a customer, a supplier or a competitor? What can you contribute to their operations and their bottom line and how can you help them achieve their own goals? Successful businesspeople are ultimately successful *people* people, with the capacity to understand and attend to the requirements of others as well as themselves.

Charlotte Jones was struggling with staff retention at the small courier company she had recently taken over from her parents. Having grown up working in the family business, she had taken over the reins suddenly when her father had a stroke, and within six months she had lost a third of her staff and was having trouble replacing them.

At the same time her father was ailing and her mother, having become his full-time carer, was barely able to look in on the business, let alone provide the mentoring Charlotte so desperately needed. As another long-term staff member handed in his resignation, she pulled him aside and asked him to be candid with her as to why he was leaving the company. He was just covering his bases, he told her, as he'd heard a rumour that she had plans to wind up the company.

That night Charlotte drafted a letter inviting all remaining staff members to an afternoon tea the following day.

She had been so busy struggling with the new business and family commitments that she hadn't realised that the staff members were unsure where the company was going, or whether they would still have their jobs in a few months' time.

Charlotte fully intended to continue to run the company; she'd worked in it all her life and could not conceive of another business or job. In the sudden and difficult leadership transition, she'd simply forgotten to tell the staff of her intentions.

At the afternoon tea she thanked them for all the work they had put in over the years, and reassured them that they would be needed to ensure that the company could continue to operate through this difficult time. She also pointed out that she intended to continue to operate the company and would be looking for opportunities to grow into new areas and invited some of the long-term staff to apply for new roles within the management of the company to help her achieve those goals.

Charlotte's candour and gratitude paid off in spades. Despite this rocky period, the company expanded its operations to three other cities within five years, and staff turnover was dramatically and immediately reduced.

Running a company can be a lonely, all-consuming activity, and it's important to find a way to regularly look at yourself the way others see you in order to understand what your actions mean to them. By attempting to see yourself as others see you, it's possible to gain a better understanding of how they will respond to you. And by putting their needs first, you're ultimately more likely to have your own needs met, or quite possibly surpassed.

Chapter 18

Taking control means keeping control

Crossing the line between being an employee and becoming an employer is challenging, and not just because it brings with it a series of new responsibilities. What you'll discover early on is that you can't be an employee and an employer at the same time.

If you've spent your life working for others, you'll be used to working alongside other people. For most of us, it's what we've done since we first walked through the gates of school, and kept on doing right through our working lives. When you run your own business, you'll still need to work alongside people, but you'll also need to work as a manager; you'll need to delegate and organise, motivate and inspire. Doing well in business necessarily means doing well with people. And running your own business means working simultaneously in a number of very different relationships.

The most dangerous person in business is not the person who tells *you* what they think; it's the person who tells *others* what they think about you. Perception is often more powerful than fact. You assume that the way you treat those around you is being interpreted in the spirit with which it is intended, but at times, even well-meaning comments can be taken as slights, let alone comments that are aimed at poor performance. This is why it's often better to play it safe, adopt a professional persona and try to put yourself in the shoes of others as often as possible.

> *Perception is often more powerful than fact.*

Never speak to anyone in a way you wouldn't want to be spoken to yourself, never hold anyone up to ridicule, even in jest, and never make a criticism personal; it should always be focused on work and outcomes. One of the biggest challenges is learning how to tell people what to do in a manner that is clear and inoffensive. For some it comes easily, but it can be particularly challenging if you're not naturally predisposed to telling people what to do.

And here's where you can get stuck between the rock and the proverbial hard place, because failing to tell people what to do can be even worse than telling them what to do the wrong way. Failing to tell people what to do, in a clear and courteous manner, is a great way to cause problems with partners and employees alike. Don't be bashful, and don't be apologetic. We're all here to do a job, and the people working alongside you will appreciate knowing where they stand and what they are supposed to be doing.

I always struggled with the idea of having to tell someone else what to do. As a young man, even ordering food at a restaurant was difficult, so you can imagine what it felt like when I suddenly found myself running a company full of capable, intelligent peers when we first took over Mineral Securities and launched it as TCG.

What I soon discovered is that leadership is quite simply the ability to convince others to do what you want them to by sharing with them a vision of where you're going and what their role is in getting there. Leadership is most successful if in fact it is a partnership, where each contributes their skills towards the same goal. This way people don't end up doing things for you because they feel pressured, but because they actually want to do it, understanding and sharing the common goal.

If you're not a natural leader, or feel uncomfortable about telling people what to do, you will just have to act it out for a while. Try to play the role you need to adopt at work in order to get things done. Just like when you were an employee, there are ways you behave in the office just to do the things that you need to get done. As a manager, you have certain tasks you need to complete—and one of them is communicating with your employees.

Being a boss isn't about being bossy; it's about being clear and concise. It's about communicating in an efficient, timely manner. If you don't express things clearly, or leave things too late, you'll end up barking orders, rather than making polite requests. Barking orders is a great way to undermine the confidence and respect of those around you. And if you think it makes you feel like a dog, just imagine how it makes you look to others.

Never shout, never cry, always be courteous and always treat others with respect. Sounds easy, but it's not. Deal with worries on your own time. Keep it inside, then go out onto the balcony when no-one is looking and let rip. Shouting and crying shows weakness; it shows you are losing control. Losing control isn't such an issue when you are surrounded by friends and family, but it's *always* an issue in the office—in anyone's office, but especially in your own. Shouting creates resentment, and no matter how liberated they claim to be, men just don't cope with crying. And even though women may claim to cope, they're just as capable of holding it against you as the next person.

Respect and recognition are the two essential elements of influence.

Just hold on those extra few moments, request an adjournment, or wait until the meeting is over, and let it all out when you're alone. You don't need to bottle it all up inside—getting twisted up and stressed is just a great way to get sick—and you certainly shouldn't go home and take it out on your family.

Businesses can be stressful to run; this is just a fact of life. As an entrepreneur it's your job to ensure you have a regular activity that keeps you sane and keeps your reaction to stress under control.

Exercise is a great way to deal with stress, and a great way to think through problems and challenges. Jogging, swimming, yoga or boxing—it doesn't really matter, as long as your body is active and your mind is free to unwind for an hour or two every couple of days. If you don't find a healthy way to manage stress, you'll end up going crazy, getting sick, losing your business and quite probably hurting a lot of people on the way.

Nick Moran runs an IT services company based out of Melbourne and Perth, called Evolve IT Australia. He began the business straight out of high school and made a lot of mistakes along the way. But the one thing he got right from the get-go was how to treat people. Respect and recognition are the two essential elements of influence. If you want to effectively influence those around you, make sure you recognise their achievements and treat them respectfully at all times.

Moran knew this almost intuitively, and when his business began to grow he surrounded himself with people he trusted and whose company he enjoyed. Job interviews were more like friendly chats than interrogations. Rather than focusing on what a person had achieved in the past, he talked with them about what they knew how to do now and what they wanted to do in the future.

He expanded the company by simply treating others the way he wanted to be treated, and focusing on developing long-term relationships with business customers and employees alike. You're not in business to make friends, but it sure helps not to make enemies along the way. As a result of his personable approach, and a lot of hard work, Moran's company grew slowly but solidly over a decade, rarely losing a staff member—or a customer, for that matter.

That's not to say, however, that what worked for Moran will necessarily work for you. You need to figure out the best way to treat people based on your own personality, and theirs. You probably know what not to do through experience, and know what to do intuitively, but putting it all into practice can still be a challenge.

Like everything else in business, managing relationships is about playing it safe and reducing risk. At the very least, if you maintain a personable and polite demeanor, and treat those around you with respect, they will enjoy working alongside you.

Listen to staff whenever possible; consider their suggestions and concerns, and try to recognise the work they have done on a personal level. Even if you don't take up their suggestions, recognise that they've been made. A few quiet words of thanks and praise are often more effective than an 'employee of the month' award. When possible, do favours for others, not because you necessarily want them returned at some stage, but because it's a great way to build bridges within your organisation, and between your business and others.

When possible, do favours for others…

We're not talking hippie 'love and be loved' ideas; we're talking about how to build respectful long-term relationships on which your business will depend. And remember, arrogance can be a very expensive approach in business. Arrogance is a blinding and powerful force, and it leads to costly, unnecessary and stupid mistakes. It is arrogance that prevents you from listening to new ideas, or suggested improvements to your company's practices. It is arrogance that will see you miss out on important opportunities. Arrogance is knowing what you don't know, and not even bothering to remedy it.

Part III

Growing with the profit principle

Dear Peter,

You are in Arad, Romania — the city where you grew up.
It is 1992. The air outside your apartment is dark grey
and the winter sky is low. You watch as cars slowly make
their way along the street below, wary of slipping on the
icy roads. Shielded against the cold by many layers of
clothing, a few unlucky souls struggle their way along the
street, evoking memories of the times you shuffled your
way down these same snowy streets to attend classes or
run errands.

Three decades after arriving in Australia, you've
returned to your homeland with a small group of investors
and entrepreneurs. The former Soviet bloc is crumbling
and you're interested to see if you can use the business
skills you have accumulated over 30 years in Australia to
acquire or launch a company in this frozen landscape.

Once, this was your home. Your name and your
family had a reputation here, built up not over a few
decades, but over centuries. People often knew you
before they met you, so tight were the circles of
commerce and the bonds of family. Your name was a
brand, and it was a brand that held a certain degree of
credibility. It inspired trust.

In Australia you have always been a foreigner. You
have had to introduce yourself, be patient and consistent.
You've had to convince others that you were capable and
reliable, and build the name of your companies, because
you could no longer depend on the name of your family.
But it has not all been a struggle: the sky in Australia is
high and bright blue, giving you the freedom to explore.

As your businesses grow from small cottage
industries into large-scale enterprises, you've begun
to understand that the difference between small and

large companies is not just a question of scale, but also a question of focus. The small company focuses on providing the service directly to the customer, but as it grows the focus of the company changes to creating the processes that underpin this service. The brand, your name, needs always to be a point of trust, but underlying that trust is your capacity to deliver services on a small or massive scale.

This isn't the first time you've returned to Romania. You've come back many times before. You've brought your children here into a landscape that is as alien to them as Australia was to you when you first walked off that boat. You've come here with other groups of people with a common background, sharing nostalgic visions of combining your success in your new home with the heartstrings that pull you back to this landscape. But try as you might (and you will try many times) you will eventually discover that your name is no longer spoken in these streets, and your brand and business, while strong on the other side of the world, simply fail to thrive in these environs.

Your challenge right now is like the challenges you faced when your businesses first began to grow beyond their first set of offices, when you first went out to recruit new staff and expand your customer base. What you will eventually realise is that your particular talent lies in creating many small to mid-sized niche businesses. You are good at finding and commercialising new technology, and so you have already created, and will continue to create, businesses with others. You will partner with large companies to get global reach for your products, and you will make small but vital components that others integrate into their own systems and carry all over the world.

You will continue to use what you know to create new companies, and you will be lucky enough to work with many talented and enthusiastic people. These people will be important to the success of your business, and you will see that there are many ways to grow a company into a successful business. Although not all small businesses will become successful large businesses, you will begin to understand what it is that limits their growth.

Soon the sun will rise over this snow-covered city and the street below will become a slushy, wet thoroughfare. People will slip over on the ground and get soaked, and drivers who fail to respect the slippery surface will slide into other cars, causing angry confrontations. Don't despair when things don't work out the way you planned. If you slip on the ice, pick yourself up and keep going.

You're never too old to learn from your mistakes, and even better, from those made by others. Hold on to what you've managed to achieve, and don't let nostalgia overwhelm you. The country you left no longer exists, and that is a good thing. The country you were hoping to return to isn't the environment you need to achieve what you want and that makes you sad. But keep in mind that there are always other opportunities; your job is to find them.

Yours sincerely,
Peter Fritz
25 July 2010

Chapter 19

Perfection is the enemy of progress

Seeing that you've got this far, it's pretty safe to assume that you're interested in making your business work for you (rather than the other way around), which is why learning where to draw the line on perfection is so important.

Most people who run their own small business wind up working harder and longer than they should, chasing unattainable levels of perfection. In fact in many cases it will be this striving for perfection that ultimately holds people back. It prevents them from taking their business to the next level, striking out into a new industry, or developing a new market.

There are numerous things that can sidetrack you and take you away from your goals and plans when you go into business. The biggest dangers lie at opposite ends of the spectrum.

Most people start out with some kind of business plan. The more organised will have this written out, complete with profit and loss estimates, fixed costs, marketing estimates—the first 18 months mapped out to perfection. Others simply start with an idea and go careering from one potential customer and supplier to the next without any real structure or plan.

Problems never arise in this initial phase, because there are no overheads, no customers, no income and quite frankly no business. Problems do arise when the customers come in, and the suppliers start sending through their own invoices. Or when the customers don't appear.

The best way to prepare for business is to be prepared to constantly change and modify your plans as your business develops, not to beautifully craft a business plan or lovingly develop a prototype and then launch it a week too late into a market that doesn't need it. Businesses work best when they are based on lots of tiny improvements rather than one large leap.

When TCG began it was a mining technology consultancy with a single product, but it has morphed over the years into all sorts of different operations. During the 1970s we had a branch called TCG Computer Inputs which provided the punch cards that computers used to require in order to function. As the technology changed, the cards were replaced with digital tape, and later with discs. We had to change and update our operations. And, if anything, the pace of this change is accelerating.

There are also times when your idea is right, but you need to work hard to find the right way to sell it, or the right person to sell it to. When Naomi Simson plunged her life savings into a web-based business called RedBalloon, she had fallen in love with the idea of selling 'experiences' through a

The best way to prepare for business is to be prepared to constantly change ...

website. She wanted to build a business based on fun and excitement. She amassed suppliers, built and launched the website, then spent months knocking on doors, handing out balloons, calling human resources managers, talking, pitching, plugging and doing her level best to share her enthusiasm for the idea of gifting experiences. And for weeks on end, nothing happened. No customers, no buyers, no income, no interest, nothing.

In this early period a business isn't even a business; it's still just an idea, and an idea that's costing money. The problem is that if you give up at this stage because what's happening in real life doesn't match your business plan, you lose the chance of ever succeeding.

Business plans, no matter how formal, need to be flexible. Your motivation to get out there and find the customers who'll turn your idea into a business needs to stay firm, while your approach, your product line and your marketing need to be sufficiently flexible to respond if the market simply isn't interested. The ability to change and respond to the customer ultimately dictates your success. That isn't to say you should give up on innovative ideas; it means you should set yourself up so that you're not killed by overheads before you can actually find that first customer.

Rather than abandoning her business because it was not aligning with her initial business plan, Simson just kept on trying different approaches. As the business was based on the web, her office was based in her home and she was her only employee, she could afford to hold out.

And in reality she didn't have to hold out all that long. Within three months she had her first customer—and no, she hadn't covered costs, but she had her first opportunity to prove the idea and create a positive reference for future customers. Customers aren't just discrete sales; they are opportunities to create more customers, either through return business or through word of mouth. Having worked in marketing for some very large and creative firms, Simson knew this and was keen to make the most of each and every opportunity. Sure, things didn't go according to her business plan initially, but she restructured it and just kept on going. Not achieving your initial goals doesn't mean you've failed; you only fail when you give up.

When you set out everything in a nice neat business plan it all looks perfect, but what you're looking at isn't a successful business—it's pure theory. When you start out in business and actually get the first few customers, then you can go back and revisit the business plan—but don't let it dictate success or failure.

Remember those black-and-white images of Wilbur and Orville Wright trying in vain to get their prototype gliders into the air? They started in 1900, with a mixture of physics, mathematics, craftsmanship and imagination. By the end of 1901 they were on the verge of giving up;

after almost two years they were still unable to balance the weight of the gliders with wings big enough to provide the initial lift they needed to get their ideas off the ground (literally).

But instead of calling it a day and scrapping the project because it wasn't going perfectly, they again hit their note-pads, recalculating then reconstructing their ideas until they came up with a new prototype with longer, narrower wings, less drag and more lift. In the process they were the first to use a wind tunnel to test their designs. Although unsuccessful, each successive failed pro- *... you only fail when you give up.* totype provided them with more information and more data they could use to actually put together a model that would take to the skies.

Even so, it wasn't until December 1903 that this series of cumulative changes would lead to the first controlled, sustained flight. Even then the predecessor of today's jumbo jet flew less than 40 metres and only remained airborne for 12 seconds.

Success in business is the same: it's never easy and it never goes according to plan, but it will be worth the struggle. Expect to take time to get your ideas off the ground, and be prepared to be constantly challenged. Expect failure, but expect to learn from it. Expect to go back to the drawing board a few times, and don't fall in love with your first design. Don't for a moment think you need to invent something entirely new or revolutionary, and don't discount ideas because they are not immediately successful, or 'perfect'.

Chapter 20

Small businesses stay small

It is clear to many small-business owners that their own role in their business is crucial to its success in the longer term. What often isn't clear is that their *vision* for their business is also important for its success. You can only ever grow as big as you can imagine being, and small businesses are most often limited by the size of their owner's imagination, and not because of other limiting factors.

Why start small and stay small? It's for the same reason that most people never start their own business at all. People who are trapped in the employee mindset are trapped in the idea that they are safer drawing a cheque from someone else each month than they are striking out on their own. Although they often have the skills to start their own company, they don't do it because they don't make the connection between the skills they have and the money coming into their employer's company.

The small-business mindset is as powerful as the employee mindset, and just as limiting. It is based around the mental image that tells you who you are and what you are doing in business. If that mental image only involves one line of products, one approach to distribution or one set of partners, then it will be impossible for you to ever break out of that mindset to see what you are in fact capable of achieving.

Five years after launching his computer repair and maintenance business, Charles Ho looked around and wondered why he was still working 12-hour days, seven days a week, for little more than a technician's salary. The business he had started with so many high hopes had become a millstone around his neck. The freedom he had envisaged had disappeared beneath reams of invoices, work orders and cleaning, insurance and repair bills. The flexibility he had visualised had long ago been replaced by the need to man the shop around the clock and do house calls to good customers on the weekends. He seemed to be forever tripping over boxes in a chaotic, poorly planned workshop, and the strategy of winning customers by offering the lowest possible price had left him working harder than ever for less money, since a computer shop offering the same low-price service had opened up across the road.

Like so many small-business people before him, Charles had committed the simple error of planning for stagnation rather than planning for growth. As a result, he'd swapped a stressful, well-paid corporate job for a stressful, increasingly poorly paid owner-operator job. You probably know a few people in the same position — in fact, you might be there yourself.

The challenge faced by almost all small-business people is that they are just that: small-business people. Many are technicians, trades- or craftspeople, and are often so focused on the service they personally provide that they fail to see the opportunities they could otherwise have to expand their operations.

The classic small-business person, the perfectionist micromanager and customer relationship expert, is exactly what is needed in the initial stages when a business is getting its first few customers and establishing itself in the market. However, that same attention to detail that ensures quality craftsmanship, great customer service and a healthy balance sheet in the first 12 months starts to weigh heavily when that same person needs to divest responsibility and customer interaction as the business

The small-business mindset is as powerful as the employee mindset, and just as limiting.

grows. The friendly boss who chats with customers and offers to make staff coffee is fabulous in the early phase of operations, but it's not an approach that can be sustained in the long term.

Unwittingly, on the day he opened his doors, Charles Ho had limited the potential of his business by adopting processes and procedures that depended on his being there and participating directly in just about every interaction associated with his shop. Rather than planning for growth and putting on new staff when required, Charles just kept doing everything himself, and cutting prices to attract more customers when things got quiet. As a result, Charles was always reacting rather than planning to be ahead of the game; he quickly became exhausted, underpaid, and he didn't have the time or energy to think strategically.

While the bulk of small businesses are started as life-style choices, even these need to be managed strategically, lest they become costly, tiresome ventures. Small-business people need to put aside time for strategic planning. If you are a small-business person, you need to take the time to work *on* your business as well as *in* your business. You need to schedule time for quiet thought, research and planning into the working week. Whether it's a couple of hours spent flicking through business magazines at the local coffee shop on a Friday morning, or a few hours fiddling with accounting software and trying out different scenarios and testing different business plans, it's time well spent.

... early success can prevent long-term growth ...

Schedule time once a week, fortnight or even once a month, just to sit back and think a little about where your business is at and where it's going. Without these sessions, which let you work *on* your business, it's easy to get stuck in a rut rather than looking for more sophisticated and productive approaches.

This is where early success can prevent long-term growth. If one approach to marketing pays off, the small-business person will be less likely to attempt other approaches, and less likely to experiment. If Charles's initial leaflet campaign and low prices hadn't worked, he might have spent more time thinking and planning. A downturn in the early phases of a business is often a great motivation for the entrepreneur to sit back and conduct a full appraisal of where the business is really heading. If Charles had encountered more hardship initially, he could have looked for partners or improved his own skills to cater to areas of higher value, and he could have created more links with the local business community in order to move up the value chain. Instead, his business strategy of price attrition (based on him working ever-longer hours) was always going to fail, if for no reason other than that customers don't value what they can get on the cheap.

Organic growth and direct involvement can only take a company so far, and five years after he started Charles was hitting up against the wall he had unwittingly built for himself. To shift into a second phase of growth, the small-business owner needs to change. That's not to say the founder of a company can't carry that same operation through different phases of growth, just that their *approach* needs to change as the company expands. Basically they need to become a different person, a person who is prepared to delegate responsibility to others.

At this stage of growth, there are two fundamental changes the small-business person needs to make for their business to become mid-sized. First, they need to hire skilled people to take some of the responsibility for running the business off their shoulders, and second, they need to trust these people to actually do the jobs for which they were hired. Hiring the right people and letting them get on with their jobs doesn't sound like such an onerous task, but many small-business owners really struggle with it. If your emotional commitment to the company you founded is really strong, it can be the hardest thing to do. In chapter 23, I go into this dilemma in more detail.

It's usually the most highly skilled technical people who find it hardest to delegate. When I first went into business for myself, I found it incredibly difficult to focus on management and leave the design and build of software to others because I was still a skilled systems engineer with a deep understanding of the technical side of the business. This became easier as the technology changed and I was forced to employ people who could do things I couldn't, just to keep ahead of the rapid change. Gradually I lost my ability to design software and so for me there was a natural imperative to move away from software design and to focus more on managing and running the company.

On the other side of it, it is very challenging to work with highly skilled people who will not delegate and allow others to make their own mistakes. Highly skilled people often become stifling micromanagers, unwilling to let their staff get on with the jobs they were employed to do, and that in itself is a problem.

This is one point again where it's important to step back and imagine yourself in the shoes of your highly skilled employees. If that were you 15 years earlier, how frustrating would it be to have your boss or supervisor interrupting constantly to demand an update on where you were and what you had achieved?

In earlier chapters I talk about why it's not a good idea to turn your hobby into your business (unless you can establish that several thousand people want to buy the product of your hobby). The other problem with turning your hobby into your business is that you almost always condemn yourself to running a small business. You go into business to do what you love, but as the business grows you will need to dedicate yourself more and more to the business of business: administration, commerce, advertising, partners and suppliers. The very thing you got into business to do becomes a distant memory. As the business grows and you find yourself doing less and less of

It's usually the most highly skilled technical people who find it hardest to delegate.

what you love, and more of the buying and selling, hiring and firing, you may become disenchanted and deliberately sabotage your own growth.

If you do want to grow into a very large business, this level of emotional engagement will not help you achieve your goal. Business is business. If you want to get emotionally engaged, buy a puppy and go for long walks with it while contemplating the strategies your business needs to get ahead, but don't fall in love with what you're doing.

For Charles, however, there was a way out. It wasn't that he was too emotionally engaged with the business—he was just too busy to think strategically. Finally, he got fed up and changed his approach. Rather than battle on in the retail space, he shifted his operations into a warehouse and opted to focus entirely on services. He traded his car for a panel van, painted it with the company logo and began to bring his computer support services directly to the customers. At the same time he approached other computer shops in the area, offering to partner and pick up subcontracting work.

This enabled him to keep his long-term customers and provided him with the flexibility the shop was supposed to have provided in the first place. It cut back his overheads and put him in touch with some of the more promising technology trends. As he began to win more work, he initially attempted to employ a technician and provide them with a van, but with information technology skills in shortage, he found it difficult to appoint staff. In order to attract staff he needed to find a way to make working for him a more attractive option, so he got creative. Rather than employing staff, he set himself up as a franchisor and advertised for computer technicians to operate franchisee vehicles. Rather than finding employees, he ultimately appointed owner-operators who had a direct vested interest in high levels of customer service, because they effectively owned their share in the business. The franchising approach also enabled him to specialise and offer services in more lucrative areas of business, and because he was offering a value-added service direct to the customers, he was no longer competing in internecine price wars with his neighbours.

Rather than continue to drown in an ever-increasing workload, Charles went sideways to go forward, creating a business model with far more potential than the retail shop he had struggled with for so long. The challenge was first to understand what he was doing wrong and realise that there was a way out — if he allowed some time out for strategic thinking and planning for manageable growth.

Chapter 21

How to be big without being big

Growing a business, like starting a business, comes down to finding and catering to customers. The main difference between a large business and a small business is that a large business either has a few big customers or a large number of normal customers. What you need to do as a small-business owner who is looking to grow is find which of those two strategies works best for you and pursue those customers.

In the commercial world there are four main routes to growth: acquisition, organic growth, the creation of intellectual property or participation in a federated system by forming partnerships with other, larger companies. Each requires different inputs and strategies, but the one fundamental requirement is that the entrepreneur must change and grow in their role as the business grows.

Many people fail to manage these changes because they keep thinking about their company the way they did when they first began, and don't stop periodically to consider whether the management styles they bring are working for the kind of company theirs has become.

Management styles from a large corporation do not simply transfer into a small business, and vice versa.

Most businesses set out with a certain approach to customer acquisition.

There are countless examples of senior executives who had failed to make their own small enterprise successful, and others of small-business people who run themselves ragged attempting to remain involved in every layer of a company that has simply expanded beyond their management style.

I've worked around these changes by looking at each new business at TCG as a new entity, and letting it dictate its own management requirements according to the capabilities of the partners and staff involved.

Most businesses set out with a certain approach to customer acquisition. They may advertise, seek word-of-mouth recommendations or use pre-existing contacts to promote their products and services, and thus grow a strong initial client base.

However, real growth requires new customers and the internal capacity to service those customers over the long term. It's easy to look at the revenues of larger organisations without taking into account the internal structures that enable those companies to sustain large revenues. The most risk-averse way of acquiring new business is simply to ramp up existing techniques, do what's worked in the past and at the very least you'll know what's coming. Answer more requests for tenders, post more advertising or seek out a new business partner and expand your business through their contacts as well.

The other way is to buy into another company, but these kinds of mergers are never as straightforward as they first appear. In a perfect world, mergers take place between companies with separate customer bases, happy staff and complementary skill sets. The resulting organisation, in theory, doubles its customer base and saves money by reducing the costs in processing and production.

However, in the real world mergers don't happen between companies A and B, they happen between real entities made up of real people — and that's where it can all become unstuck. Mergers can often lead to drops in productivity, as staff and customers question their allegiance to the new operation. Sales can fall away, and the costs of combining two separate companies often run way over any predefined budget. Small companies tend to take over other small companies, specifically to take over their customers in a single hit rather than win them over painstakingly one by one. The idea is to ramp up productivity, increase customers and reduce costs, but the complexities and costs of mergers are often underestimated.

Mergers and slowly acquiring new clients are the most obvious path to growth, but both are slow and fraught with difficulties. If growing very large very quickly is your end goal, the most effective way to go about it is to focus on the creation of intellectual property, and to partner with a very large company and piggyback on their infrastructure and distribution channels. Large companies already have access to large numbers of small customers or small numbers of large customers, and have already set up the distribution systems you need as a small company to get your product off the ground.

The trick to working with a much larger company is to make it worth their while, while not pricing yourself out of the picture. There are numerous examples of small entrepreneurs who stay small despite having a novel product to take to market. Many fall down somewhere along the path to commercialisation, rather than in the initial development stage, because the path to the customer is more treacherous than the path of innovation. Because distribution partners are a route to many customers, they need to be treated like one very big and very important partner, and the key to success lies in fitting into their existing practices.

Stop for a moment and ask yourself if Bill Gates would ever have been able to launch Microsoft if it weren't for the fact that IBM decided to adopt his QDOS operating system for its personal computers. Would Frank Lowy ever have become Australia's richest man without joining forces with major retailers David Jones and Woolworths? No-one, in life or in business, survives in a vacuum, which is why it's important to remain aware of those around you, what they have, what they need and how your business might be able to operate in conjunction with theirs.

But remember that, like customers, these potential partners do not owe you their business. In the same way that you owe the customer the favour of supplying a good or service in the right place at the right price, the same goes for distribution partners. The best way to deal with them is to offer to make their lives and businesses simple and straightforward. Don't go to a potential distribution partner expecting them to give you anything; go with an offering that will fit into their model.

Growing means finding customers, and finding customers often means working with large distributors. The challenge when it comes to large distributors lies in actually convincing them to work with you in the first place. The distributor is in effect a new customer to whom you need to sell both ideas and goods. Like all partnerships, distribution arrangements need to be based around mutual interest, and in the case of a small company catering to a much larger company, the onus is generally on the smaller company to make itself relevant to the larger one. Most small companies find it difficult to be relevant to large companies because they focus too much on what they are bringing to the relationship, rather than on what the larger company would gain from the relationship.

No-one, in life or in business, survives in a vacuum...

But size, although tempting, may not necessarily be what you need, and you may spend months courting an impossible relationship while letting other opportunities slide. Before you approach potential partners, you need to know how big you're actually able to grow. Being big is risky, especially in a small market, and often it is better to create slow, steady growth rather than sudden spurts.

This is where having the time to think strategically becomes so important. You, as the head of your own company, need to spend a lot of time considering your surrounding environment, and looking for potential partnerships. Talk to everyone. Don't filter people on the basis of who they are today, because people move and change. Take time to network and to create an extensive list of business contacts, because if you want to grow you need to find the right sorts of opportunities, whether they be partnerships, acquisitions or distribution deals.

Chapter 22

Don't stare at the horizon just to trip on the road

There are plenty of books out there that will tell you that in order to create a successful business you need to have a vision—a plan. Once you've got that, you need to keep marching resolutely towards the horizon to achieve your vision. But nothing could be further from the truth.

Sure, it helps to have a long-term goal—as long as you're prepared to change it constantly as circumstances change and opportunities arise, and as long as you're prepared to keep focused on the task at hand rather than staring at the horizon.

If you stare at the horizon as you progress, you are quite likely to trip on the way. It is possible to start a business with no capital or debt, as long as you're willing to look at the world from a slightly different angle (preferably not off into the distance), and re-assess regularly. Look at your business as a collection of paying customers, and seek the active participation of others, rather than frittering away any money you already have on establishing the business of your 'vision'.

Oddly enough the same thing I've been hammering home when it comes to starting a business can also be applied to expanding a business, either organically through increased sales, or by finding a complementary company and taking it over. It doesn't have to take money to get off the ground.

Possibly the best way to acquire something for no money is to find something that is not worth much to its current owners. If you look around and keep your business contacts up to date, you'll discover that there are plenty of those opportunities lying around.

Many businesses expand by committing the mistake of buying into a company when it's already for sale, or buying into a sector when it's already booming. This is a great way to make the seller rich, and leave yourself heavily in debt. The most promising businesses are never overtly for sale, whether or not they are making the owners any money.

Take the example of Integrated Wireless. This is a communications sales company that is part of the TCG Group, my company, and it's currently a very profitable venture. But this wasn't always the case. When we first came across the company we were very concerned that we would not be able to turn it into a profitable business—after all, the existing owners had been losing money on the venture for many years.

It operated initially as a sales office and Australian outpost for a much larger international company. The division had not made any money for five years, despite a healthy turnover and demand for its products. Subsidiaries are like small businesses that start out with a lot of cash: they are always in danger of failing because they start out in an unrealistic mindset of being able to spend money before they make it. Integrated Wireless in Australia had fallen headlong into this trap.

The most promising businesses are never overtly for sale...

Nonetheless, the owners were not looking to sell initially. While they weren't happy with the company's operations, they were resigned to the idea that it would simply continue to operate as an outpost that made a loss.

What made Integrated Wireless an interesting option for us at the TCG Group was that we could see how, with a few modifications to the way the company operated, it could become a very profitable venture, sell more product, and make more money for the owners, whoever they may be. But it had to make the transition from being the small sales arm of a larger company to being a separate business that operated profitably in its own right.

These initial negotiations took about a year to conduct, and it was important to secure the support not only of the business's owners, but to also find an internal sponsor for the sale. We needed someone in senior management to support the transition; otherwise we risked losing the staff.

It turned out that the challenge for the larger company was that, while they had a lot of faith in the Australian market, they were not sure how to make the sales division operate profitably, and it was groaning under the weight of onerous and time-consuming reporting practices. All of the reporting practices were necessary for the larger company to keep a track on its outpost, but they also detracted from the profitability of the smaller entity.

Sometimes being aligned with a bigger company works in your favour, but in this case it was working against the company's success. Eventually the original owners agreed to part with the company for the price of $1, having been convinced that indeed it could be worth more to them if it were separated from the parent company. The price was remarkable, but their motivation was entirely understandable. For years they had been pouring money into a venture that seemed totally incapable of turning a profit. It was costing them money to run, and would have cost them still more money to close down as they would have had to cancel contracts and pay out staff. It was sold to us with negative cash flow and significant overheads, and the hope was that by turning it around we would actually make the parent company money by selling more of their product.

Taking the company from loss to profitability was not a straightforward process, but we were equal to the task. The very first thing we had to do was to ensure it began making money, and quickly. We began by going over the company's operations, determining who the best sales and support staff were, cutting costs and increasing incentives to sell. Where possible, we deferred payments to suppliers, renegotiated the terms of many of the supply arrangements, and moved into less expensive premises.

Most importantly, we stripped away much of the administrative paperwork, so that the good salespeople could go out and sell, and the good technicians could go out and repair stuff without worrying about having to come back to the office to fill in forms.

There are benefits and challenges associated with all businesses, no matter what the size. It's important to always work within your constraints rather that wishing for something that you don't have. Small businesses need to be agile, and in removing the red tape, Integrated Wireless immediately benefited from increased agility.

The very first thing we had to do was to ensure it began making money, and quickly.

Salespeople were able to get out and sell, the administrative staff was able to spend their time supporting the sales staff, and within six months the company made its first midyear profit in five long years.

Profitability was the first major hurdle we needed to overcome. The next step was for us to begin to take a closer look at what the company had internally, and what kinds of options existed for expansion. Within the company we discovered a talented technical support team. We spun it off into a separate company, providing its technical staff with more training and expanding its customer base into new areas. We appointed leaders within the company who would manage effectively and passionately, and let them get to work.

Within three years, the sales had doubled. It was at this stage that the company could get down to creating some serious value and begin to develop its own intellectual property. The more highly trained technical team began working on software, which could ultimately be sold in the local market and also back into the company's international division.

The added revenues gave the company the opportunity to buy into premises and expand its branch office network. Within six years, the company consisted of several divisions including sales, technical support, research and development and facilities management. It owned two buildings, and, remarkably, had not lost any staff across its network. But it would have been impossible to predict this kind of success when we first purchased it.

... it's so important to keep your eyes resolutely on the road ahead.

The only way it managed to get this far was by the leaders involved placing one foot in front of the other and moving slowly forward, making sure each step was solid before advancing further. Profitability had to come before investment, investment before expansion, expansion before new facilities and so on in a chain that seems clear and simple in retrospect, but has to be taken slowly, deliberately and in a very specific order.

There's not a business plan, mission statement or company vision in existence that deals with all possible scenarios, which is why it's so important to keep your eyes resolutely on the road ahead. The horizon might be tempting, but you'll never actually make it if you trip up on the way.

Chapter 23

Find the right people and let them get on with their jobs

Growth can be a double-edged sword for many business owners. As businesses expand, the owner requires an ever-changing series of capacities and capabilities. The skills you will need as the leader of a very large business are different from the skills you need to manage a mid-sized business which are different again from the skills you require as a small-business person or an employee. You need to either constantly update your skills and your role in the business or be good at finding the right people to fill the roles that you can no longer deal with yourself.

Growth is a little like going through your first pregnancy. You become so wound up and focused on the growth strategy that you tend to forget that it needs to be followed up with a new management strategy. There are plenty of first-time parents who read every book in the library on pregnancy and labour, then get home and have no idea what to do with the newborn baby. Focusing on the growth rather than the management may leave you with an overwhelming, sticky, noisy mess.

The small-business manager needs to be involved in their business at all levels. They need to know everything from profit and loss summaries to fixing the coffee maker, and the sort of people who do well working in a small business tend to be tactical rather than strategic thinkers; people who are good at getting stuff done with a minimum of fuss. There are companies that are perfectly suited to this type of management: restaurants, cafés and other shopfront or retail businesses need managers with the capacity to actually get down and cook the meals, talk to staff and customers, place ads in the local press and clean the toilets if need be.

The leader of a large organisation, on the other hand, needs to understand how to create long-term strategies and goals, and how to inspire staff to work toward the same goals. Once a business grows beyond about 15 staff members, it becomes impossible for the owner or manager to continue to have such a hands-on role within the organisation. As the business grows, small-business managers need to overcome their urge to be involved in every single aspect of the business.

The tactical staff members, so fundamental to the initial stages of a small business, are still fundamentally important, but what a mid-sized company also needs is a layer of competent strategic managers, who can organise and inspire.

The role of the entrepreneur is to always sell the business, whether it's by organising partnerships, winning tenders or creating distribution arrangements. The main connection the entrepreneur has is with the outside world, and this connection needs to remain intact as the business grows. This is why you need to figure out how to find and keep good staff before you grow. In order for your business to grow, it's necessary for the business to run without your direct input.

And here's the secret that small-business owners and a lot of mid-sized-business owners seem never to learn: you can measure people's output without sitting on them all day. In fact, micromanagement is the best way to create resentment and reduce productivity. Creative, intelligent people like to be left alone and be trusted in what they are doing. As such, your role as a manager is to find these people and then leave them alone to get the job done, while you go out to win more business.

The role of the entrepreneur is to always sell the business...

This approach of stepping away from the day-to-day operations of the business to focus on strategy and marketing becomes increasingly important as the company grows. But it can be a little like watching your adolescents grow up and take on a little independence; you can't exactly be peering over their shoulder and watching every move, but you do need some way to ensure that you will find out in a timely manner when things are going wrong. The key here is to set up self-checking mechanisms that will keep ticking over most of the time, and alert you when something is going wrong in the early phase.

This is also the growth phase where you need to focus on who you hire and what they will bring to the company. Small or mid-sized companies that employ poorly skilled staff and don't invest in workplace development are doomed to remain small or mid-sized. Growing businesses need smart, flexible people who are committed to the company and happy to take on different sorts of roles when need be. Integrated Wireless, the company that TCG bought for $1, is a perfect example. Freed of the reporting requirements of the larger company, the staff members felt a greater sense of responsibility and control. Working within a smaller organisation, they were able to take *Organisations* charge of the company's destiny and *with a low staff* within one year we were able to turn a *turnover rate grow* basket case into a sustainable business. *more quickly...* In three years we doubled the turnover and were able to produce steady, consistent profits. We almost doubled the number of staff working there, and expanded to new cities. Most importantly we were able to use the company's existing business to develop a line of software, which is now exported back through the original parent company into markets all over the globe.

Your staff members are your business partners—without them, your business does not exist. Still, many business owners treat their staff as some kind of parasite, sucking profitability out of the business. In well-run businesses, with good staff, the opposite is true. By seeing staff in terms of costs rather than revenue generation, these employers fail to enable staff, and therefore the company—which, after all, is built on the skills of the staff—can't realise its full potential.

Recruitment is an enormous drain on resources, and it's often cheaper to pay people slightly more than the market average and create a workplace where people actually want to be than it is to be forever looking for new staff. The extra wage is largely symbolic; it sends a message that staff members are important. That message is more important and relevant than the actual amount, and the message needs to be backed up in other ways to ensure that it gets through.

Organisations with a low staff turnover rate grow more quickly because their resources aren't being constantly drained by recruitment and staff members find it easier to communicate and trust each other more because they have worked together for an extended period. Staff members who have worked together for a long time are also often more productive, especially when working in teams, because their communication tends to be better and their roles more clearly defined as each project is being carried out.

Small businesses stay small, and mid-sized businesses stay mid-sized, often because they fail to attract good staff—or fail to keep them if they actually manage to recruit them in the first place. Like customers and partners, employees will only get involved in your business if you make it worth their while. Like customers who need great products and services, and business partners who need great opportunities, employees need some kind of fundamental motivation to get involved in a business and stay with it in the long term.

Here's the big secret that most businesses fail to understand about employees: they are not primarily motivated by money. If they were, they'd be in business for themselves. Employees are motivated by security and by the opportunity to come into a workplace where the work is enjoyable and challenging (and where they are treated well). Simple things like doing an orientation on the first day, or ensuring that the new recruit can begin immediately by making sure they have a computer and a phone line ready to go on the day they start, can make a huge difference.

Good employees will shop around until they get the best offer, and most will happily forgo cash incentives for the right working conditions and environment. By trying to compete on price rather than focusing on the benefits they can offer as employers over and above large businesses, small- and medium-sized businesses put themselves at a disadvantage. Focus instead on what makes your business the best place to work. An important thing to realise is that an interview is like a sales pitch: you need to explain why the employee would want to work for your organisation, as much as you need to find out whether or not they would be suitable.

Small- and medium-sized businesses also often fail to do the sums on creating flexible work practices for employees who are starting a family, or who for whatever reason need to take some time off. Getting good people back again from maternity leave is much cheaper than finding and training new staff. Creating work practices that enable people to work from home or job-share will enable you to keep good staff and transfer skills across a small team. Another benefit of fostering a flexible workplace is that you provide staff with a tangible reason to come back to work, tomorrow, next week and next year.

As the business owner, it is your job to welcome new staff as much as it's your job to meet with potential clients. It's important to take a few moments with them early on and communicate the company's goals and values, and also offer them a chance to come back to you with ideas as to how they might fit into that vision. It's also your job to work strategically on recruitment. Staff members will stay with you if *Good employees will shop around until they get the best offer...* they see a future for themselves within your company. It's worthwhile conducting annual reviews, not only to see how staff are developing, but also to ask specifically what they are hoping to achieve and look at ways to get them there.

Good staff members will forgo all kinds of perks and payments just to work in a company where they feel they have a future, and the businesses that win the recruitment game are mostly those that take the time to communicate that future to potential recruits.

Getting the process of recruitment right is a fundamental precursor to growth, and poor recruitment will often undermine growth. If you are planning to grow rapidly, you need staff members who feel confident and empowered to make decisions based on their own skills and training. Hire smart people and give them a chance to do their job and they will stay with you and grow as you do — taking the company beyond the small, into the midsize and ultimately into the realms of the very large.

Finding good staff and keeping them is the only way to create a large company—and regularly losing staff is a great way to ensure that your business will stay small long into the future. The choice is yours.

Chapter 24

The bicycle balance

Wow — you're really determined to see this one through! That's good, because if you've come this far I can safely assume it's been of some value to you (or at least it will be once you get a chance to put all the ideas into action). At this stage I hope you'll have started thinking about business not in terms of fixed business plans and investment capital, but in terms of customers, partners and employees. The thing to remember is that these approaches weren't created in a void — they are the result of decades of actual hands-on experience in business. They weren't created by someone who always got things right either — in fact, a lot of them came about because I went wrong somewhere along the line.

Starting is always the hardest part, but finding that first customer isn't the end either. Finding the first customer is just a stop en route to finding a second customer, just as launching an initial product or service is just the first move.

Running a business is like riding a bicycle: if you stop, you fall over. Running a successful business means finding ways to integrate all the different skills and demands placed upon you into a series of eight-, 10- and often 12-hour days. But if you think that running a business necessarily means excluding all other activities then you're very much mistaken. There's no point in creating a business to have more flexibility and more time with your family, only to find yourself locked in an office 12 hours a day. There's no point in building a business around your skills base and then working yourself into the ground.

Once you've launched your first project, you already need to be thinking about how you will manage your next project: what will it cost and who will buy it? You will be thinking a number of months ahead. Where will the income come from? How many calls do you need to make in order to stimulate a single order? Will it be 50 calls to get one order? Or just 10? Is it worth putting on more staff to cover your existing workload—and will you be able to find enough follow-up work to keep them on afterwards?

Business doesn't happen at a single point in time; it happens over an extended period. Every day you'll make decisions regarding how to stimulate the inflow of business, how to manage the outflow of cash, and how to ensure that you're getting the most from the investments you're making in staff and services.

But there's another critical element that many business-people forget: YOU. That's right—if you're going to run your business you need to ensure that you are fit and well and capable of getting out of bed tomorrow. After all, if you're not there, there will be no business to run.

Like many people I largely ignored my health and the role exercise could play in my business until it was, in some ways, too late. It wasn't until I was diagnosed with type 2 diabetes that I began to pay very careful attention to my diet, and then only because it literally had become a matter of life and death. And it wasn't until I broke my leg in a canyoning

Running a business is like riding a bicycle: if you stop, you fall over.

accident that I began to pay particular attention to the amount of exercise I got each week. I now go to the gym at least twice a week to build up a sweat, and regularly lift weights. What surprised me was that rather than making me tired and lethargic, the exercise gave me more energy and a clearer mind, and left me more capable during the day.

I'm sure that if I had discovered a way to integrate regular exercise into my daily routine in my younger years I would have been able to stave off the type 2 diabetes as well, but it's too late now to complain.

Many people get this balance wrong because they see the business side as somehow removed from the rest of the tasks they carry out each day. You'd like to get more exercise, see your family more or eat better food, but because you see it as somehow separate from the business of your business, you don't actually factor it into your day. Well, here's another little secret: your business depends on you being fit and healthy and, just like employee reviews and strategic planning, exercise, family time and a healthy routine need to be integrated into your schedule.

Many busy people mistakenly think that putting aside time to exercise each morning (or even just a couple of times a week) is somehow unproductive, but nothing could be further from the truth. Taking time each day to exercise not only enables you to bring more energy and a clearer head to the challenges you face, but it will also provide you with some all-important down time—a chance to think through different plans and come up with new ideas.

... your business depends on you being fit and healthy ...

A number of major organisations are integrating physical activity into their daily routines because it has been found to increase productivity and reduce absenteeism at all levels of the workforce. This gets us back to the bike idea. Exercise programs usually fail because people see them as separate from the business or businesses they are running. But in order to continue riding forward, you need to find a way to integrate all of your business requirements into a single path.

That path is as much about keeping you healthy as it is about keeping your balance sheet healthy. There won't be any point in starting a business in the first place if you don't take care of yourself, because you simply won't be well enough to enjoy the ride.

Chapter 25

There's no beginning, there'll be no end

Think for a moment of chapter 2 where I show you how the best businesses don't actually have a clear-cut beginning, and why it is important to look for organic ways to grow one business out of another. I've talked about why businesses only come into being once there are customers walking through the door and spending money, and why growing your business will always come back to your capacity to find customers (rather than your capacity to spend money on making your business look and feel like a business).

Now that we're reaching the tail end of the book, it's probably also time to deal with the tail end of the company, and the point at which you decide that your business is no more. While your business only comes into being based on your capacity to bring in customers, your business will only ever stop functioning when you stop looking for customers. Your career as an entrepreneur is entirely based on your capacity to find people who will pay you to do whatever it is your business does.

No true entrepreneur ever fails, because no true entrepreneur ever gives up. At any given time you might be more or less successful; at any given time your ability to attract customers might be better or worse; but your business and your entrepreneurial career only stop when you do.

In 2010 Andrew Forrest was widely considered one of the most successful businessmen in Australia. Thanks to the success of Fortescue Metals, the iron-ore mining operation, Forrest is one of the richest men in Australia—but less than a decade ago he was being pilloried by journalists and institutional investors for having failed to deliver on a high-tech nickel mining project called Murrin Murrin. A partnership he'd won with mining companies Anglo American and Glencore had collapsed, and he was branded a liar by many in the mining community.

No true entrepreneur ever fails, because no true entrepreneur ever gives up.

That same year, several million other businesses collapsed around the world, and several million small-business people and entrepreneurs found themselves scratching around looking to rebuild their careers. You might even have been one of them.

In business 12 months is a long time, and the only difference between Forrest and the million or so other entrepreneurs who failed in some way that year, but then didn't recover is that he picked himself up, dusted himself off and kept on going. Angry, hurt and dealing with a reputation that was in tatters, he nonetheless kept on seeking out opportunities and customers. In 2003 he took complete control of a company called Allied Mining and Processing. He knew mining, he knew the region of Australia called the Pilbara, and he knew that the only way to stay in business was to find more customers.

He renamed Allied Mining and Processing, calling it Fortescue Metals. His target was the rapidly expanding market in China for iron ore. His approach was to invest in the infrastructure that would make it as inexpensive as possible to ship vast quantities of red dust and turn it into steel.

This time around, his plan was successful. So if we decide to end the story in 2010, Andrew is a wealthy mining entrepreneur. If we had stopped the story in 2002, he would have been a failed mining magnate. What Andrew understands is that his business only stops when he does.

Your business only stops when you stop looking for customers, no matter how big or how small. Your idea only fails when you stop looking for ways to make it a success, which is why it's so important for you to look for ways to grow your business without overheads and without going into debt.

As long as there's more money coming into your company than there is going out, you'll be successful. Begin by finding a customer rather than being a customer and you're off to a great start. Grow by finding a partner, rather than finding a contractor, and you'll grow more quickly. Expand by appointing franchisees or partners rather than finding staff and you'll create a self-perpetuating momentum that will be easier to sustain and grow than any business that relies on you, as a boss, to be looking constantly over the shoulders of employees who aren't interested or engaged in any meaningful way with your project. If you've got a business that relies on staff, make sure you invest in keeping them happy and letting them get on with their jobs.

The ability to pick yourself up and dust yourself off and just keep on going is the one thing that separates successful entrepreneurs from failed businesspeople. And the ability to ensure that your company can always pay its bills is key to ensuring that you have the opportunity to continually reinvent yourself and take on new opportunities when they arise.

The very best businesspeople know this intuitively, and as a result they're able to learn from their failures and build constantly on their successes. The most risky decision you will ever make in business is to decide to spend money you haven't already made, or to pay for products and services that haven't already been paid for in some way by forward orders and contracts. First find your customers, then find your suppliers, then build your business.

Forrest is not the only example of a businessperson who has gone to the brink of failure or come back from a significant setback. Keen sailor and enthusiastic philanthropist Graeme Wood also tried his hand at all kinds of different businesses for two decades before happening on a business idea that would propel him into the status of multimillionaire. A systems analyst, he spent the early part of his career studying the way businesses function and reinterpreting those processes into software. He developed this skill into a series of different software businesses with varying degrees of success throughout the 1980s and 1990s, but it wasn't until 2000 that he decided to use a web-based hotel booking tool to connect discounted hotel rooms with weary travelers and launched Wotif.com.

Wood had 20 years' experience using technology to connect customers with services, and a technical background of analysing business processes in order to reinterpret them as software processes. This certainly helped Wood and his partners turn Wotif. com into the successful business it has

First find your customers, then find your suppliers, then build your business.

become, but that's not the main reason it was successful. The main reason Wotif.com did so well was that Wood and his associates were in the right place at the right time, with the right skills. And the reason he was there was that he simply refused to stop doing business.

Your business is just the same. What you are currently working on may not turn out to be the phenomenal success you are hoping for, but don't let that stop you from trying again. You may have been forced to close or sell out of a business that you had invested time and money and boundless enthusiasm in. But don't let any of that stop you trying again—just don't be silly enough to try exactly the same approach again. Learn from your experience and learn from your mistakes, and take that knowledge into an entirely different venture. As long as you keep your overheads low and your company debt free, you will be able to experiment with any number of different approaches.

When he was making his comeback from the failed nickel-mining venture, Andrew Forrest told the media that he'd learnt to choose his partners more wisely and to create a corporate structure that would discourage takeovers and therefore minimise distractions. Following a not-so-successful venture into trading agricultural goods on the internet in the 1990s, Graeme Wood said he learnt to stick to the area he knew, which was information technology and services.

The only person who will stop you from succeeding in your next venture is you …

Both were right. They used failure to plan for success. And here's a secret they know intuitively: the clock doesn't stop when your business fails. It keeps on ticking, and there's nothing to prevent you from getting up, dusting yourself off and starting again.

In the same way that businesses have no clear-cut beginning, neither do they have a clear-cut end. A business that goes bankrupt may no longer be able to pay its bills, but chances are it was trading while insolvent for some time before anyone noticed. And the fact that one venture has failed does not prevent you from becoming involved in another — in fact, it places you in the perfect position to learn from the experience and to make sure that your next attempt is more successful.

Ultimately there are no failed entrepreneurs. The only person who will stop you from succeeding in your next venture is you, and the only way you'll fail is if you fail to learn.

Final thoughts

Now we get to the end of our journey. Creating a business out of what you already know, finding partners and working with others, respecting the talents and skills of those around you, looking for opportunities to grow and thrive—these are some of the many separate elements of creating a successful business. But to create the picture of how it all comes together, we need to start at the forest floor.

Seems like an odd and entirely inappropriate place to start, but unless you understand how it all begins, you'll have a hard time understanding how it'll grow. You see, it's easy to run a business the hard way. It's easy to come up with an idea, throw huge amounts of money at it, bulldoze a plot bare and plant your perfect forest. But you might find that what you've planted is completely unsuitable for the climate and environment, and it soon withers away. It's actually more challenging, but will pay off far more in the long run, to first take the time to look at what's around you, and to figure out how to plant what you want to so it can find a place among what is already growing around you.

Imagine for a moment that you are sitting on the forest floor, surrounded by shrubs, leaves and fallen timber overgrown with moss and fungi. Above you is a multi-storey canopy: great arching branches covered in clouds of leaves of different shapes, sizes and colours. Spindling their way above the lower shrubs, saplings stretch out and up, their growth kindled and encouraged by the towering giants of the upper canopy.

Stop and think for a moment about the business world.

Stop and think for a moment about the business world. Think of the huge multinational companies whose presence stretches out far from their origin. Think of all the large companies with huge workforces and vast research and development budgets. Think of their suppliers and partners, from the guy who runs the café through to the vast manufacturing works where they source their components.

At the very highest point of the forest canopy only the leaves and upper branches of the tallest trees bend in the wind. Small animals and birds range across the branches and nest in the ancient hollows in their trunks. Leaves from the trees fall, making their way to the forest floor, or are eaten by animals. Here they mix with minerals from the earth, trapping warmth and air, absorbing water and enabling bacteria to flourish. It is this underlying humus fuelled by billions upon billions of bacteria that enables the shrubs and saplings and trees—everything—to grow.

At any given time, a single apex tree both supports and depends upon four or five saplings, a dozen shrubs, five or six types of fungi, a metre or so of decomposing leaf matter, thousands of earthworms and billions of bacteria. And that's without figuring in the participation of the birds, reptiles, insects and other animals that keep the system ticking over by pollinating, eating, digging and carrying seeds from one spot to the next.

Most of the saplings won't grow into vast trees, and even the largest, oldest tree will eventually fall and be consumed again into the forest floor, but at any point in time there are thousands of different species all inhabiting the one small patch of earth, all depending on each other for sustenance.

No business operates in grand isolation, just as no tree grows on its own. From your shady spot on the forest floor, take some time to look around and see how each element of the forest interacts with the others. How the minerals of the soil and the frequency of the rainfall determine which species find a foothold and which fail to get established, how the existence of the single apex tree encourages smaller plants, but prevents other larger trees from growing too closely together.

Look at which plants flourish, and how they interact with the other species. The fungi grows slowly along fallen branches after a wet spell, the shrubs do well but struggle for room as the conditions encourage hearty competition, and the saplings, while protected from the elements, grow slowly in the shade. Each element adapts to its surrounds, and grows within given constraints.

Though glorious in its native surrounds, a maple will fail to thrive in a semi-arid zone where the soil is thin and the rains scarce. A pawpaw tree will grow apace in the warm wet tropics, but die in the cold of the European winter. An ancient eucalyptus tree might stretch more than 20 storeys in a naturally dry region, anchored by deep, water-seeking roots, but keel over in the wind in damper, more fertile soil. So it is in business.

Each element adapts to its surrounds, and grows within given constraints.

The underlying nation is your mineral base, your bedrock. Its regulations, education system, traditions of corporate governance and physical infrastructure are the elements that make up the topsoil. It may be rich and dense with opportunities. It may provide a wealth of speculative investment, venture capital, a well-educated professional class and strong regulatory environment.

Some environments support only a small selection of species, such as an arid, semi-desert region, where stunted, bushy shrubs predominate and the odd tree struggles skyward. Others support a jungle of plant and animal species, predators and prey all trying to outdo the other with showy displays and verdant foliage.

But don't make the mistake of assuming that the desert is devoid of possibilities, or that the jungle is an easy environment in which to survive. Some economies support a wealth of different businesses without giving them the opportunity to truly flourish. In others it may be more difficult to get started, but the chances of success on a grand scale are better in the long term.

The largest trees obviously take the longest time to establish themselves, just as the largest and most stable companies are usually passed down through several generations. But they also support a range of symbiotic species, each of which draws on their success. Around the base of the tree a dozen or more saplings might be inching their way skyward, but only one or two will be there in the long term. On the other hand the lichen and fungi that grow over the bark of the larger tree will be there, even when it expires and falls to the ground.

Now, come back from the forest floor into the present business environment and look around you.

What do you see? What kinds of businesses already exist? How do they relate to the other businesses around them? How suited are they to the regulatory environment? Do they grow slowly, or have they expanded rapidly? Do they thrive by growing over and strangling other businesses, or do they complement those around them?

Understanding business means understanding a whole ecosystem of dependencies and interrelations, and succeeding in business comes down to understanding which ideas will thrive and which will fail given the pre-existing environment.

In Mexico taco stands thrive. Government regulations regarding street stalls are flimsy and rarely enforced, and the population loves the product. While their yields aren't all that spectacular, they play an important role in keeping a hard-working population fed on the way to, or home from, work. They exist not because of the intrinsic human need for tacos but because of the intrinsic human need to work and to eat. More importantly they exist because of the cultural, economic and political climates that enable them to exist.

In Australia, where street vendors are by and large prohibited except for in and around malls and markets, and regulations on food preparation are somewhat stricter, it costs a lot more to establish an equivalent fast-food outlet. As a result the Australian business world is bereft of taco stands. But it has its own equivalent: the suburban kebab shop. Similar to the taco stand, the kebab shop sells meat and vegetables wrapped in flat bread, but it costs more to run, employs more people and makes more money, at the end of the day, than the Mexican taco stand. The set-up and running costs are higher, risk is higher, and returns are higher.

Understanding the business ecosystem also means understanding the supply relationships on which your business will depend. Take the trousers you're wearing. They came to you through a crisscross of national and international business relationships that certainly rival the forest ecosystem in terms of complexity and interdependence. Though simple in appearance, the trousers would never have graced your legs had it not been for the particular specialisations of a raft of businesses, each at once feeding into and depending upon each other. The retailer, whose very existence depends on the tradespeople who build and maintain the premises, the utilities that keep it lit and comfortable, the till and accounting system, and the education system that produces literate, employable staff. The distribution system, which hauls crates of garments off international cargo ships and matches them with the relevant retailers, the import/export agents, the sailors and shipwrights, the translators and salespeople that grease the wheels of international trade. The cutters, sewers, wrappers and carriers slaving away at the point of production, the chemists who make the dyes and the fabrics, the metal agents who make the zippers and clasps, the miners who bring the metal out of the ground, and the processing plants that turn that metal into all manner of tiny devices. The designers, managers and organisers who operate within every business have to source this raw material, accumulate the human and physical capital and create the connections between input and output. All this and more just to get a pair of trousers. You can only imagine what sorts of inputs are required for still more complex products.

But this isn't about getting dressed. It's about thinking more deeply about the interconnected and ultimately symbiotic nature of the economy. It's about looking for opportunities not only to start a company, but to found a company that will thrive in the existing conditions. It's about seeking out relationships, and about working *with* and not *against* the pre-existing conditions to make your business idea into a success. It's about finding your place in the world and working with what you have rather than lamenting what you lack.

Look around. What do you see?

Index